Your Towns and Cities in the Great War

Southampton
in the Great War

Your Towns and Cities in the Great War

Southampton
in the Great War

John J Eddleston

Pen & Sword
MILITARY

First published in Great Britain in 2014 by
Pen & Sword Military
An imprint of
Pen & Sword Books Ltd
47 Church Street
Barnsley
South Yorkshire
S70 2AS

ISBN 978 1 78346 296 4

A CIP catalogue record for this book is available from the British Library.

Designed by Chapter & Verse Designs

Printed and bound in England

Pen & Sword Books Ltd incorporates the Imprints of Pen & Sword Aviation, Pen & Sword Family History, Pen & Sword Maritime, Pen & Sword Military, Pen & Sword Discovery, Pen & Sword Politics, Pen & Sword Atlas, Pen & Sword Archaeology, Wharncliffe Local History, Wharncliffe True Crime, Wharncliffe Transport, Pen & Sword Select, Pen & Sword Military Classics, Leo Cooper, The Praetorian Press, Claymore Press, Remember When, Seaforth Publishing and Frontline Publishing.

For a complete list of Pen & Sword titles please contact

PEN & SWORD BOOKS LIMITED
47 Church Street, Barnsley, South Yorkshire, S70 2AS, England
E-mail: enquiries@pen-and-sword.co.uk
Website: www.pen-and-sword.co.uk

Contents

Introduction

The city of Southampton, which it became in 1964, has a long and proud history and has played a major part in many of the foreign campaigns that England and Britain have fought.

It was the Norman Conquest that first made the town into a major port. The capital of the country at the time was Winchester and Southampton was the closest port to that capital. From that time on, Southampton was one of the chief ports of the country. A centre of imports and exports and vital for commerce, Southampton was, on the darker side, also notable as the place that brought the Black Death to England in the mid-fourteenth century.

Being a major port on the south coast, the town was also important in time of war. During the English Civil War, Southampton was a Parliamentary stronghold and though Royalist forces attempted to take the city, they failed. Later in history, Southampton was of crucial importance for the embarkation of troops to the Napoleonic Wars, the Crimean War and the Boer War.

The town saw other major historical events. The Pilgrim Fathers sailed from Southampton in 1620 and, of course, Southampton's name is forever linked with the terrible tragedy of the *Titanic* in 1912. Many of the crew of that ill-fated vessel came from Southampton and around one third of all those who perished came from Southampton. It is not surprising, then, that the town suffered so badly from the loss of the 'unsinkable' *Titanic* and that monuments to the event can still be seen there.

It should come as no surprise that when hostilities broke out between Britain and Germany in 1914, Southampton would once again come to play a major role. Though it is true that there was a good deal of fighting in the Middle East and Africa, the main theatre of war was the European mainland. From the very outset it was clear that troops would be needed in France and Belgium and in order to get those troops to where they were needed, along with all their equipment and supplies, a south coast port would be required. Southampton was immediately designated Port Number One, underlining its importance in the eyes of the military and political authorities.

Of course, no one could know in the late summer of 1914 that the war would last so long. At the outset, many people believed that the fighting would be over by Christmas. Had that been the case then perhaps Southampton would only have seen around 100,000 troops pass through the port but, once it became clear that this would be a long, bloody war of attrition, then the city authorities knew that Southampton would play a major role in supplying men and equipment for the war effort. In fact, once the fighting was finally over, the Town Council announced that between August 1914 and November 1918, no fewer than 7,000,000 men, over 820,000 horses and mules, some 14,000 guns, 110,000 vehicles, and 3,500,000 tons of stores, supplies and ammunition had been sent to France from the port of Southampton. The port had handled a total of more than 16,500 ships and it must be remembered that this represents only what was sent to France. Southampton also sent troops and equipment to other theatres of war and these figures also do not include all the men who survived the war and were sent back to England through the same port.

At the end of the war there were hundreds of ships that sailed from Southampton to repatriate soldiers of the British Empire to India, Canada, Australia, New Zealand and other countries.

On a more personal level Southampton played a vital role in the war effort. There were many families who supplied three, four and more sons to the various branches of the armed forces. There were regular flag days and fund raising activities for such worthy causes as hospitals, comforts for the men in the front line and to provide ambulances for the Red Cross. There were even collections, later in the war, to raise money to buy a tank! League tables of this fund raising in the major towns and cities throughout the United Kingdom were published and Southampton was always to be found towards the top of those tables, usually only beaten by cities such as Glasgow and Birmingham, which had much larger populations.

There are stories of many small towns supplying men to the army and who were formed into the so-called Pals Battalions, many of which were to suffer terrible losses in battles such as the Somme. It must be remembered that, being a port, Southampton supplied many men to the navy and they fought in such battles as Jutland, the greatest naval engagement of the war. Others served on supply ships and hospital ships and they suffered heavy losses, especially to the German U-boats.

Many other men went into the infantry regiments, especially the

Hampshires. That regiment fought in many battles, including Messines, Ypres, Gallipolli, Polygon Wood, Cambrai, and Passchendaele. In total the Hampshire Regiment lost 7,580 men, many of whom were sons of Southampton and the surrounding areas. The Hampshires were awarded a total of eighty-two battle honours, along with three Victoria Crosses.

Finally, it was during the Great War that, for the first time, a new dimension was added to the weaponry; that of the aircraft. Men from Southampton also fought, and gave their lives, in the new aeroplanes, adding their own names to the many that would appear on monuments after the fighting was over.

It is a truism that almost every city, town, village and hamlet sacrificed something in the war of 1914 to 1918 but few gave as much as Southampton. Without the efforts of the people, and the facilities of the port and city of Southampton, there was little possibility that Britain and her allies could have faced the onslaught of the Central Powers and the war might well have been lost.

In many ways, we can say that Southampton played a crucial role not only in the war effort but also in the final victory of November 1918. It is a proud record and a proud history.

Chapter One

1914 The Summer of Peace

The year 1914 started full of hope and contentment. January was a month that saw Southampton receive only twenty-three per cent of the expected average rainfall. Readers of the local newspapers discovered that the first steamboat had passed through the Panama Canal on the 7th and, one week later, on the 14th, Henry Ford introduced a new concept to his factories, that of the production line.

February may have kindled many sad memories in the city when on the 26th the *Britannic* was launched in Belfast. She, of course, was the sister ship to the ill-fated Titanic, a ship that had sailed from the port just two years before and whose maiden voyage had ended in such tragedy.

The *Britannic*, sister ship to the *Titanic*. She became a hospital ship during the war.

WHITE STAR LINE R.M.S. "BRITANNIC" 50,000 TONS.
LAUNCHED FEB 26TH 1914.

The month of March saw a small, perhaps insignificant news item which stated that on the 14th, Turkey and Serbia had signed a peace treaty. This was of little interest to the people of Southampton but those two countries would feature heavily in news stories of the coming years.

April was a month for culture. The 11th of that month saw the premier of George Bernard Shaw's *Pygmalion* in London and two days earlier, on the 9th, the first ever colour feature film was shown *The World, The Flesh and The Devil*.

If April was for culture, then May was for politics and Southamptonians read that the House of Lords had rejected women's suffrage on the 6th whilst the House of Commons had passed the Irish Home Rule Bill on the 25th. Southampton, though, had more local events to celebrate, as this month also saw the May Day parade.

Part of the May Day parade in Southampton in 1914.

Another picture of the parade.

Some of the costumed characters in the May Day parade.

The parade passed through the city centre on the way to Southampton Common. An enormous throng of people gathered along the route and the choir of St Mary's sang from the battlements of the Bargate. Other entertainments were also available and, for example, patrons could visit the Carlton where *A Circus Girl's Romance* was playing. A thriller, the climax of the film was a tremendous boiler explosion at sea as a liner sank.

In the middle of the month the SS *Vaterland*, the world's largest liner, called at Southampton on its maiden voyage from Hamburg to New York

The parade marching through the town. Soon many soldiers would parade down the same street on their way to the docks and embarkation for France.

The German ship the *Vaterland* at Southampton before the war.

and on Saturday, 30 May, a large crowd assembled at the Royal Pier to witness the departure of the Hampshire Royal Garrison Artillery for Cliff End where they were to undergo their annual training.

June was a month of excellent weather and the sun shone brightly as Viscount Haldane, the Lord Chancellor, opened the new University College on the 20th of the month. Four days later, on the 24th, HMS

Safeguard was launched from Messrs Day and Summers' yard. Four days after that, an incident took place in Sarajevo, 1,033 miles from Southampton, which was to effect an entire generation.

Early on Sunday, 28 June, the Crown Prince of the Austro-Hungarian empire, Archduke Franz Ferdinand, and his wife Sophia, were in Sarajevo when a grenade was thrown at their car. The Archduke was able to deflect the grenade, which exploded behind the vehicle, injuring a number of people. Franz Ferdinand and his wife insisted on visiting the injured in hospital and then ordered their driver to take them on to the palace. Unfortunately, the driver took a wrong turn and ended up on a side street where a nineteen-year-old assassin named Gavrilo Princip was waiting. As the car started to reverse out of the side street, Princip saw his chance. Drawing his revolver, Princip shot Sophia in the abdomen and the Archduke in the neck, severing his jugular vein. Both were dead by the time they reached the hospital.

Though few people in Southampton would have suspected it at the time, the summer of peace was over.

Gavrilo Princip, the man who shot the Archduke.

Archduke Ferdinand whose assassination in Sarajevo sparked the First World War.

Chapter Two

1914 The Path to War

After the assassination of the Archduke, events took a rapid turn. On 5 July, the German Kaiser promised the Austrian Emperor the full support of Germany if Austria decided to take action against Serbia. Eighteen

Kaiser Wilhelm II.

days later, on 28 July, the Austro-Hungarian government sent an ultimatum to Serbia and on the following day, 29 July, Belgium declared that, in the event of a war in Europe, she would remain neutral.

The Royal Pier, Southampton.

In that same month, the citizens of Southampton carried on with life as normal. At the beginning of the month, one hundred schoolchildren returned from a delightful weekend in Cherbourg on the steamer *Vera*. Shortly afterwards, Laurence Legge, a former Southampton resident, returned to the city to star in *"Hullo Everybody"* at the Hippodrome and on 21 July, the Earl and Countess of Northbrook visited Southampton to open the annual carnation and sweet pea show on the Royal Pier.

In Europe, the rush to war continued unabated. On 25 July, Serbia began to mobilise her troops. The following day, Austria-Hungary did the same. Two days later, at midnight on 28 July, Austria-Hungary declared war on Serbia and Belgrade was bombarded on the 29th; the first shots in the war.

Despite its declaration of neutrality, Belgium mobilised its forces on 29 July but things moved even more rapidly in August. On the 1st of that month, Germany declared war on Russia, an ally of Serbia. That same day, France commenced mobilisation.

On 2 August, Germany sent an ultimatum to Belgium demanding that it should be granted free passage through Belgium in the event of war with France. That ultimatum was refused on 3 August and on the same day Britain guaranteed armed support to Belgium if her neutrality was

Belgian troops at the Battle of Liege.

violated, in line with her treaty obligations.

The fateful day was 4 August. It was on that day that German troops crossed the Belgian border and attacked the ancient city of Liege. Britain stood by the promise she had made, and at 11.00 pm declared war on Germany. Eight days later, on 12 August, both Britain and France also declared war on the Austro-Hungarian Empire. The conflagration that would be called The Great War, or World War One, or even The War to end all Wars, had begun.

Chapter Three

1914 All Over by Christmas

Southampton heard of the declaration of war at 12.45 pm on Wednesday, 5 August. Hundreds of people assembled in Above Bar and the announcement was greeted with loud cheers. This was immediately followed by the throng joining in a rousing chorus of the National Anthem, followed by the Marseillaise in support of our French allies. There were repeated calls for cheers, first for the French and Belgian governments and people and then for Admiral John Jellicoe, a native of

John Jellicoe, a son of Southampton, who was appointed supreme commander of the Home Fleet in 1914.

the city, who had been appointed the Commander in Chief of the Home Fleet on the day war had been declared. The crowds did not finally disperse until around 2.00pm.

It was just one week later, on 12 August, that the first real event of the new war impacted on Southampton. A German vessel, the SS *Hanna Larsen*, had arrived at Southampton with a cargo of timber from Archangel in Russia. When the war had commenced, the crew had left their ship and tried to return to Germany but could not get out of England. They duly returned to Southampton, only to find that their ship had been seized by customs officers. The crew themselves were then arrested and spent the rest of the war in prison in Winchester. The *Hanna Larsen* would later be used as a coal transport vessel by the British, based in Newcastle-upon-Tyne. She would be sunk, in 1917, by a German U-boat.

The authorities realised that Southampton would have a major part to play in the war. It was a major port, handy for crossings to France and Belgium and at the outbreak of hostilities it was designated No 1 Military Embarkation Port. Much of Southampton Common was taken over by the military and there troops would assemble, prior to being shipped out to join the British Expeditionary Force. It was, of course, early days and the war had only just begun but, by the time it was over, a total of

Troops boarding ship at Southampton for embarkation to France.

Another picture of troops and their horses boarding ships bound for France.

8,149,685 troops, of many different nationalities, would pass through Southampton on their way to war. Many others would return to the city wounded.

One of the horses leaving a ship in France.

This was all for the future. The patriotic fervour continued in the city. Mr G Colman Green caused a good deal of attraction in Above Bar when he arranged for a large map of Europe to be painted above his shop, his intention being to mark the position and movements of the various armies involved in this war, which would surely be over by Christmas.

It was clear to the general public that Southampton would be the major port for the departure of troops to France and other possible theatres of war and the local population were eager to show their support for the forces. In mid-August, the local newspapers carried reports that Southampton ladies were busy doing Red Cross work and were busy making blankets for possible hospital use. On Monday, 13 August, no fewer than 200 ladies were based in the Victoria rooms, sewing blankets by hand.

Many men enlisted in the first weeks of the war and some families supplied many sons to face the foe. For example, Mr and Mrs Harding, of Station Road, Romsey, had six sons, all of whom were now in the forces. Even young children played their part. Bobby Coxwell, just four years old, who lived at 63 Shirley Road, sold badges in aid of the Prince of Wales Fund, and raised the sum of £6 13s 6d.

Just one of the patriotic families who sent more than one son to war. These are the five sons of the Hallum family. From left to right:- Wesley, Howard, David, Stanley and Reuben.

There were, however, items of bad news. One of the first Southampton casualties of the war was Lieutenant K.F.B. Tower of the Royal Fusiliers. A prominent yachtsman, well known in the town, he was wounded in mid-September. At about the same time, the press reported yet another patriotic family, Mrs and Mrs George Hallum of 9 Carlton Crescent, who had supplied five sons to the forces: Wesley, Howard, David, Stanley and Reuben were now all serving their country.

Many of the young men who joined up in Southampton, rather naturally perhaps, found themselves in the various battalions of the Hampshire regiment. It was the 1st Battalion which first saw action.

The early months of the war were ones of fluid movement by the opposing armies. The first real battle, for the British, opened on 23 August, when the Germans attacked the Franco-British forces at Mons. The allies retreated and on 26 August, the Hampshires were heavily involved in the Battle of Le Cateau where Corps of the BEF fought a rearguard action to slow down the Germans whilst the rest of the army continued to retreat.

The Germans seemed to be doing very well and soon were approaching Paris. Once again the Hampshires were involved in the Battle of the Marne, which opened on 6 September. The French, with British support, stopped the German advance and then launched a counter attack that pushed the enemy back. The battle continued until 10 September.

On 13 September the German forces managed to stop the Allied counter attack at the Battle of the Aisne. This battle lasted until 15 September and ended in a stalemate. The first trenches began to appear and, once again, the Hampshires were involved in the battle.

Although the southern area of hostilities now largely consisted of two massive armies facing each other in trenches across a scorched no-man's land, the area to the north was still fluid. There began a period which became known as the 'race to the sea', where both armies tried to gain control of the Channel ports. Part of this scramble was the battle of Messines which began on 12 October. Yet again the faithful Hampshires were involved in the fighting which lasted until 2 November.

HMS *Aboukir*, on which George Walton died when she was struck by a torpedo from the U9.

By the time the battle was over, trenches had appeared in the north and the lines now stretched from the Belgian coast all the way to Switzerland.

As the war progressed, further tragic reports came to be published. In late October it was announced that George H. Walton had been drowned in the sinking of HMS *Aboukir* on 22 September. He had previously served 21 years in the navy and had been in the reserves for two years. He obtained employment as a postman at the main Southampton Post Office and was called up just before the outbreak of war. He left a wife and five children all of whom were under twelve years of age. Two other ships, HMS *Cressy* and HMS *Hogue* had come to the assistance of the *Aboukir*, thinking that she had hit a mine. In fact, *Aboukir* had been torpedoed by the U9 and the submarine now picked off the other two ships. A total of 62 officers and 1,397 ratings lost their lives.

For many, though, life went on as normal. It was also in late October that the newspapers published a picture of two Indian soldiers at the railway station. They were amongst many Empire troops who would come to defend Britain in her time of need. The reporter who interviewed them said that they had complained of it being rather cold but added that otherwise they were very happy.

Though the local Hampshire regiment was not actively involved, 19 October saw the opening of another battle, one which would last until 22 November. For many people who read the reports in the Southampton newspapers, it was the first time they would ever have heard of an obscure Belgian town but it was to be a name that many would remember in the years to come. The name that the press articles carried was that of Ypres.

In Southampton, in November, the naval and military authority confirmed that they would permit the public to let off small fireworks until 8.00pm on Guy Fawkes Day. Next to this announcement was an advertisement from Cox and McPherson of 62 High Street, stating that they had for sale boxes of fireworks ranging in price for 1d to £1. Later

HMS *Hogue*, another ship sunk at the same time as the *Aboukir*.

that same month a remarkable story was told. A soldier named A. Rapp, who had been a photographer before the war but had joined up immediately hostilities were declared, was lying badly wounded in a hospital in Calais. He had been wounded in Belgium but had then lain in the mud for twenty-nine hours before he was rescued by a member of the RAMC. Coincidentally, the medic who found him and saved his life, was also a native of Southampton.

No less a remarkable escape occurred the following month, December, when Trooper Stanbrooke, another native of Southampton, was hit by four bullets. The first had smashed the top of his bayonet, passed on and hit him in the thigh. The second had struck his pocket knife and tobacco pouch and caused him no injury. The third had bounced off a button in his tunic and the fourth and final bullet had struck him in the hand. He, too, was now recovering in hospital.

By December it had become clear that this was going to be no quick war over in a few months. It was going to be a long and bloody affair but, even now, there remained signs of basic humanity.

In the days leading up to Christmas, there had been efforts to bring some peace to the lines. One hundred and one British women, members of the Suffragist movement, had signed a letter 'To the women of Germany and Austria', asking for peace over the forthcoming festive season. A more official communication had come from the new Pope, Benedict XV, who pleaded for an official truce between the armies over Christmas. There was to be no official truce but some units, including the 1st Battalion Hampshire Regiment, did take part in a remarkable unofficial one.

There are many stories of the Christmas Truce of 1914. In some parts of the line there was no temporary halt to the shooting but in other areas, including those guarded by the Hampshires, singing broke out in both the German and British lines. Carols and Christmas songs were heard in both English and German. Small makeshift Christmas trees appeared in some places and were planted above the trenches. In places soldiers tentatively made their way into No-Man's Land and exchanged greetings with their opposites. Gifts were exchanged and there was even a spontaneous football match between the British and the Germans. The French troops took little part in the truce and the entire episode would be played down by the government, claiming that nothing of the kind had taken place.

The truth is that along the trench lines where the British and German forces faced each other, there were many incidents of the ordinary soldier forgetting, at least for a couple of days, that the men opposite were enemies, intent on destroying each other.

The Christmas Truce of 1914 was never repeated on a large scale; very few incidents took place in the Christmas of 1915. By then the two armies had come to distrust each other and events of 1915 would show just how horrific this war was to become. It was never again to be one in which ordinary soldiers could, for a time at least, forget that they were at war.

Chapter Four

1915

January

By the beginning of 1915, it was clear to most people that this was going to be a long war. It did not begin well. On the very first day of the New Year, 1 January, HMS *Formidable* was sunk by a German U-boat off the coast at Lyme Regis. Out of a total complement of 780 men, thirty five officers and 512 sailors lost their lives.

Still, morale was high and the newspapers carried uplifting news as well as the darker items. One early report referred to the children of the Central School in Southampton. Over the Christmas holidays the school premises had been used to billet soldiers who were to sail from the docks to France. The children had kindly left a chalked message on one of the blackboards, welcoming the soldiers and wishing them well. The soldiers had responded by leaving their own message, thanking the children for their good wishes.

At about the same time, around a hundred soldiers sat down to an excellent tea at St Barnabas's church. By all accounts they had enjoyed a splendid time and thanked the citizens of the town for their kindness and consideration.

The blackboard messages left by the children of Central School and the replies from the soldiers.

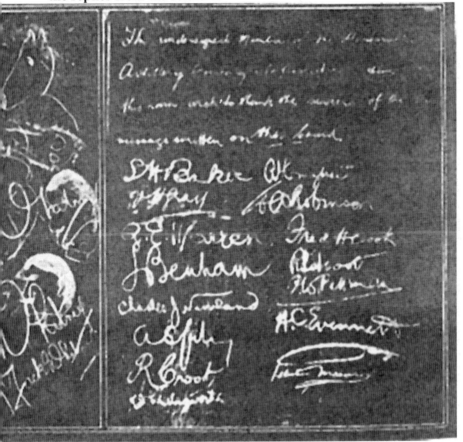

'A' Company of the 5th Hampshires in India.

Fundraising and charity continued unbounded. Early in the year the British Ambulance Committee handed over a number of vehicles to the members of the French Red Cross Society, for use at the front. The official handover was made at the Royal Hotel.

In January pictures of the 5th Hampshires were published. They were

A group of sergeants from the 5th Hampshires relaxing in India.

The 5th visiting an Indian temple.

based in India and the newspapers showed photographs of men visiting Hindu temples, though the articles referred to them as Hindoo. Officers were shown with a goat they had been given as a mascot and it seemed that all were having a most enjoyable time in the sub-continent.

Not such a good time was apparently being had by Captain William Thompson, a well-known local yachtsman. Before the war he had been employed by a German company and had spent a great deal of time in many of the German ports. At the outbreak of hostilities he had been arrested, possibly due to his phenomenal knowledge of the ports, and was now being held in a German camp, where he would spend the rest of the war.

Better news followed towards the end of the month when, on the 24th, the Battle of the Dogger Bank took place. This proved to be a victory for

'C' Company of the 5th, also in India.

A silk postcard sent from Southampton to one of the men serving at the front.

the British fleet and the German armoured cruiser *Blucher* was sunk. Only fifteen British sailors lost their lives in the action. More ominous news appeared in a small article, which referred to a confrontation on the Eastern front, where no British forces were involved. At the Battle of Bolimov, the Germans had used a new weapon on their Russian foes. That weapon was poisonous gas and it would play a sinister part in future stories from the Western front.

There was news too of local casualties. Perhaps one of the saddest was the announcement of the death of Stoker Thomas Brown, originally from Dorset but then of 27 Mount Pleasant Road in Southampton, who had been one of the 736 men who died when HMS *Bulwark* exploded on 26 November, 1914, near Sheerness. It was believed that cordite charges had been kept too close to the boilers and the resulting explosion had blown the ship to pieces.

February

Large numbers of postcards and letters passed between the British soldiers fighting around the globe and their friends and families back home. Many of those sent by soldiers at the front at this time, were quite humorous, perhaps reflecting the morale and attitude of the Tommy. Later in the war, darker postcards would be sent, many of them showing the destruction of towns in Belgium and the results of war on the landscapes.

Patriotism still filled the newspapers. Sapper Fielding Rundle was awarded the Distinguished Conduct Medal for his action at Ypres the previous year. He had been operating a field telephone when a barrage of shells exploded near him. He was wounded by shrapnel in both legs, his right arm and his side but had continued his work. A native of Southampton, he was now recovering in hospital at Bath.

Families who had supplied more than one son to the forces were honoured. Thus, for example, people read of the Tatum family of Shirley Road, who had three sons in the army. One was a lance corporal, one a staff sergeant and one was a driver and all were serving at the front.

It should be remembered that British soldiers were not only serving in France. Other local men were based in India, Egypt and other parts of Africa. One of those areas of operations was around the Suez Canal where, on 3 February, the Turkish army attacked in force. Fortunately, they were beaten off with heavy casualties.

The War Cabinet, which planned attacks in the various theatres of war, decided that it would be a good idea to force Turkey out of the war at the

The Germans were also sending humorous postcards at this time. This shows a German soldier disposing of a British, French and Russian opponent.

earliest opportunity. The plan was to capture the capital and, in order to do so, the Dardanelles would have to be forced, using naval power. With this in mind, on 19 February, ships shelled the forts guarding the narrow straits. By coincidence, this was the 200th day of the war.

One other event, reported at the beginning of the month, would have far reaching effects later, not just for Britain but for the entire course of the war. On 4 February Germany announced that in future she would engage in unrestricted submarine warfare. From now on, any ship heading to or from Britain was to be considered a legitimate target, even if that ship were flying the flag of a neutral country; it was a policy that was soon suspended but was resumed a year or so later.

How the newspapers reported the Indians fighting at Neuve Chapelle.

March

The patriotic fervour continued in March. One of the early reports was of yet another local family, this time that of Mr and Mrs Hartnell of 25 Harcourt Road, Bitterne Park. They had no fewer than six sons serving in the forces, one of whom, Frederick, was a survivor of the *Titanic* sinking in 1912. Frederick had been a saloon steward and was rescued in Lifeboat 11, one of the most heavily laden boats launched from the stricken ship.

Another sailor, Alfred William Randell of 86 Derby Road, was not as fortunate as Frederick was in 1912. Alfred was serving as a cook's mate on board HMS *Amethyst* which was one of the ships engaged in the attacks upon Turkey in the Dardenelles. On 14 March, the ship was shelled by a shore battery near Kephez Point and a number of sailors, including Alfred, were killed.

In fact, it was largely the navy in the news in March. In addition to the above stories, readers also discovered that on the 10th, HMS *Ariel* had managed to sink a German submarine, the U12; and the following day, 11 March, the British fleet started a blockade of German ports. Not all the news was good, however, for on 18 March a joint British and French fleet began the final bombardment of the narrows through the Dardanelles, in preparation for a later land based attack. Three British ships were damaged and three more, HMS *Irresistible,* HMS *Ocean* and HMS *Bouvet* were lost. It might well have been seen as a sign of things to come.

As far as the war on land was concerned, March saw the first major British attack of the year around

Neuve Chapelle. A joint venture between troops from Britain and India, the first shots were fired on 10 March and the fighting continued to 13 March. It was, tactically, a British success but they failed to press home their advantage. Large numbers of German prisoners were taken, however, and many of these were brought back to Britain through the port of Southampton. Many people lined the streets as the men were marched from the docks to transports which would take them to camps around the country.

April

The month began with the news of the deaths of three local men. The first of these was that of Private Henry Edward Andrews, who lived at 86 St Andrews Road. He was killed on 14 March but the news was only now being published. He was killed at Neuve Chapelle

The second fatality was Lance Corporal Cecil Charles Beare, the son of Charles Edward and Annie Clara Beare. They had all originally lived in Brighton but, prior to 1914, had moved to Waterloo Road in Southampton.

Perhaps the greatest publicity was given to Private Frederick John Jones, born in Southampton who had, before the war, worked as a conductor on the trams and lived at 12 Belvidere Terrace in Northam. He too was killed in action, on 15 March, and now lies in Brown's Road Military Cemetery, Festubert.

The first major confrontation of the month was covered in the newspapers in late April, for on the 22nd, the Second Battle of Ypres began. This was not an Allied operation but a massive German attack which would last until 27 May. It

Private Jones, the ex-conductor on Southampton's tramcars, who was killed in action.

involved the extensive use of poisonous gas against British troops for the first time and the 1st Hampshires were heavily involved in the defence of the line.

Three days later, on 25 April, the first Allied landings at Gallipolli took place. Troops from Britain, France, Australia and New Zealand were involved and what would turn out to be a complete fiasco would last until January of the following year. As far as local interest was concerned, troops of the 2nd Hampshires were involved, landing at Cape Helles. On the day after this, 26 April, Italy joined the war on the Allied side.

The month also saw the last playing of the FA Cup until after the war. Southampton had been beaten in the third round. After drawing 2-2 with Hull City at home on 20 February, they lost 4-0 in the replay at Hull on 27 February. The final itself took place on 24 April, Sheffield United beating Chelsea 3-0 at Old Trafford in Manchester.

May

Without a doubt, the biggest news story of the month was the sinking of the *Lusitania* on 7 May. The Germans had announced the policy of unrestricted submarine warfare in February.

On the outbreak of war in August 1914, the *Lusitania*, a British ship, had been commandeered by the Admiralty for use as an armed merchant

How the *New York Times* reported the sinking of the *Lusitania*.

The *Lusitania*, sunk by the Germans and which greatly angered the United States.

cruiser but it was quickly realised that she was unsuitable for that purpose, so she was allowed to continue as a passenger liner, providing she also carried government cargo.

On 1 May, the ship left New York, bound for Liverpool. By 7 May she had reached a point some eleven miles off the southern coast of Ireland and it was there that she was attacked by a U-boat, the U20. As the ship started to sink a second, internal, explosion erupted and the vessel vanished below the waves in eighteen minutes, with the loss of 1,198 lives, 128 of whom were American citizens.

It was true that the German authorities had paid for a newspaper advertisement in America advising the citizens of that country not to travel on the *Lusitania* as it was considered a valid target but, as far as the American people were concerned, this had been a non-military ship and Germany had broken the rules of warfare. Though it would be two long years before the decision was finally made, it is certain that this event played a large part in later American involvement in the war.

In Southampton, the beginning of the month saw a massive recruitment rally at which one of the speakers appealing for men to join up was Lieutenant General Sir Robert Baden Powell, who founded the scouting movement some years before. By all accounts the event was very successful and many men signed up.

In the second two weeks of the month, two British attacks were launched and these were well publicised in the Southampton newspapers. Both attacks were in support of French troops who had launched their own attack, which the Germans had repulsed, causing very heavy French casualties. So, in order to take the pressure off their allies and take German troops away from that sector, Britain had launched an attack at Aubers Ridge on 9 May, a struggle that was to last two days. This was followed on 15 May by an attack around Festubert where the fighting would last until 25 May.

During the reports on the bloody fighting at Aubers Ridge and Festubert, a small item appeared, on 14 May. It appeared that the Kaiser's garter had been removed from Windsor Castle. The Kaiser had been admitted to the ancient order of the Knights of the Garter in 1901 and now, after almost a year of war, his membership was annulled.

A more poignant announcement appeared at about the same time. Private Alfred George Tierney was killed at Ypres on 23 April whilst saving the life of an officer. Though Alfred had lived in Kent and was a soldier in the 1st Battalion of the Queen's Own Royal West Kent Regiment, he had been born in Southampton and his sister, Mrs Andrews, still lived in the city, in Dover Street. Alfred was just nineteen when he died.

On 19 May, a massive Turkish attack at Gallipolli was beaten

Private Tierney, of Dover Street, Southampton, who died heroically saving the life of an officer.

off by troops from Australia and New Zealand. On the 25th, domestic troubles erupted for the government. There had been much criticism over the way the Liberal Prime Minister, Herbert Asquith, had been handling the war. He now formed a coalition government to bring in fresh talent from all political parties. Perhaps one of the most significant new appointments was that of David Lloyd George as Minister of Munitions. It was now his job to see that the armed forces had the equipment they needed to win the war.

June

June was a relatively quiet month on the pages of the Southampton newspapers. Much was made of the fact that many women were now being employed in munitions factories around the country. In fact, women were doing many jobs previously the domain of men as, of course,

Teresa Collet, a nurse killed whilst attending to the wounded at the front.

many men had now joined up and were fighting in France.

Two local deaths made news. The first was that of Private William Henry Wells of 5 Shayer Road in the city. He had been a soldier in the 1st Hampshires and was killed in the battle of Festubert on 21 May. William left a wife, Sarah, and four children. The other death was that of Miss Teresa Collet, who was only 21. She was a Red Cross nurse and had been tending the wounded at the front when she lost her own life.

One other piece of local news would have made the residents of Belgrave Road in Portswood very proud. It was announced that the road was, arguably, the most patriotic one in Southampton. There were 134 houses in the street and no less than 108 residents were serving as soldiers or sailors.

July

July began with some good news for Southamptonians to read. On the 9th of the month, German South-West Africa surrendered to South African forces led by General Louis Botha. In due course Germany would lose all her African colonies but this was the first to fall to the forces of the British Empire; German forces in Tanganyika, then a German colony, were the last Germans anywhere to surrender in 1918.

In Southampton, Alexandra Day was a very wet affair but still many ladies were positioned around the streets of the city selling roses in order to raise funds for local hospitals. Despite the inclement weather, a good deal of cash was received.

On 15 July, the National Registration Act was introduced. Up to now the various appeals for men to join the forces had proved to be very successful but the government realised that some form of conscription would eventually have to be implemented. The Act meant that all eligible men now had to register for National Service.

On 19 July, the British had had a major success in Flanders when they captured the hamlet of Hooge, near Ypres, from the Germans. A large mine had been detonated in the area and Hooge was seized without many casualties on the British side. On the penultimate day of the month, 30 July, the Germans launched a counter attack using a terrible new weapon, the *flammenwerfer* or flamethrower. Known to the troops as liquid fire this weapon, in conjunction with machine guns, mortars and hand grenades cost the British dear and Hooge was recaptured by the Germans.

Some of the new female tram conductors reporting for duty.

In fact, very few deaths were caused by the liquid fire but the effect the weapon had on morale was devastating.

August

The German success at Hooge was relatively short-lived. On 9 August, the British attacked again and the trenches so recently vacated were recaptured. Meanwhile, in Southampton, the war effort continued. The first batch of female tram conductors entered training and the first women workers took their places on the trams at the end of the month.

Many recruits from all over the country were still being sent to Southampton for transport to the continent and there were numerous parades of men through the town. Many columns of men passed under the historic Bargate, usually singing patriotic songs as they marched through the streets to the cheers of the local population.

On 6 August the newspapers carried details of another landing at Gallipolli. British troops were landed at Suvla Bay and amongst them were the 1/8th Hampshire (Isle of Wight Rifles) and the

Fares Please! One of the new conductors handing out tickets in training.

A picture of Bargate. Many troops marched through the ancient gate on the way to the docks.

10th (Service) Battery. Both units had many sons of Southampton amongst them.

September

On 18 September, the people of Southampton read that an enterprising gentleman, dressed as Charlie Chaplin, had attended the football match at The Dell to collect money for the Winter Comforts Fund, which was to be used to provide basic comforts to the local Territorials. Shortly after this, they could also read of a most heroic exploit from an airman whose family lived at West End.

In late August, Squadron Commander Arthur Wellesley Bigsworth was flying near Ostend when he spotted a German U-boat. Despite there being heavy fire from shore batteries and the submarine itself, Arthur descended to around 500 feet and dropped bombs on to the craft. Though he could not absolutely confirm the sinking of the U-boat, he did see it go under the water stern first. For this gallant feat in single-handedly sinking a submarine, he was awarded the DSO.

There were news reports that some soldiers from the Hampshires were busy training in the New Forest area and a small item referred to the army

New recruits training somewhere in the New Forest area.

testing the prototype of a new weapon, which had been named Little Willie. Manufactured by Messrs William Foster and Company of Lincoln, the new weapon, once deployed, would become better known as the tank.

Towards the end of the month, a new British attack was launched on the Western Front. Opening on 25 September, the attack took place at Loos and witnessed the first use of poison gas by the British. The battle would last until 18 October.

October

There was much to interest the reader in the month of October. On the very first day, large numbers of Fokker aircraft were deployed over the trenches. This particular aeroplane had developed a system whereby machine gun fire could be directed through the revolving propeller. This instantly gave the Germans air superiority, a state of affairs that was to last until the Spring of 1916.

There had been many rumours that Bulgaria was contemplating entering the war on the German side. In order to discourage this, British and French troops had landed in Salonika on 5 October to support Serbia and thereby threaten Bulgaria. The decision had little effect for, on 14

October, Bulgaria did indeed enter the war. The allies were now fighting Germany, Austria-Hungary, Turkey and Bulgaria.

There seemed to be a lot happening in Southampton itself too. On the 13th a concert took place on the Royal Pier in aid of the Anglo-Russian Hospital Fund. Outside the theatre a group of six young ladies: Florrie Day, Doris Lanham, Gladys Lanham, Marjorie Day, Ena Living and Kitty Day, sold programmes, flags and scented artificial flowers and in doing so raised £5 for the fund.

There was another great recruiting rally on the old cricket ground, where Sergeant W H Brandon led the appeal for fresh recruits. Later the same week the first women took up positions as bus and tram conductors in the city.

Perhaps the strangest story was of a local hero who was awarded the Iron Cross! The hero in question was a cat named Waller. He had saved the lives of two people who lived in rooms over one of

The six young ladies who sold programmes, flags and flowers for the Anglo-Russian Hospital Fund.

the banks in the city centre. One evening the bank caught fire and Waller had woken the occupants above the bank by leaping up at the window. The following day one of the bank's customers, as a joke, made an Iron Cross, which he "awarded" to the cat for its bravery.

A sadder story concerned four local men, all of whom were officers in the Hampshire Regiment. The four men were all captains and in 1911 had won the Inter-Company Polo Cup in India. Now, three of them were killed in action. Captain Caryl Lermitte Boxall was the first to die, on 27 April. Two more, Captain Owen Heathcote Lacy Day and Captain Basil Stewart Parker were killed on the same day, 6 August, and are listed in Twelve Tree Copse Cemetery. Only Captain Smith was still alive and he was wounded in the Dardenelles campaign.

There can be no doubt, however, that the major story of the month concerned an event that took place in Belgium on 12 October. It was on

Another picture taken at the time Southampton was filled with troops.

that date that the Germans shot a British nurse, Edith Cavell.

A native of Norfolk, she was working in Belgium before the war. When hostilities broke out she was in England visiting her mother but returned to Brussels soon afterwards to resume her duties. When Brussels fell to the Germans in November 1914, Edith began sheltering British, French and Belgian soldiers whom she then helped to smuggle back to England. On 3 August, 1915, after she was betrayed by a Frenchman, Gaston Quien, she was arrested and charged with treason. Found guilty she was shot by firing squad at Schaarbeek, Brussels at 7.00 am, on 15 October. The story of her execution was widely used by the British authorities for propaganda purposes, especially in the United States.

November

Initially, things had gone well for the British and Indian forces in Mesopotamia. They had had a number of successes against the Turkish or Ottoman army who had been in a constant retreat ever since they had entered the war. That state of affairs was about to change.

The main reason for the campaign in the region was the protection of the oil wells at Abadan, in modern Iran, and in fighting off the Turks, the allied forces advanced towards Baghdad. By 22 November, only a relatively small British force had been left to guard the town of Kut whilst the rest of the army reached a place called Ctesiphon. The weather was very bad but the British Commander-in-Chief, General Nixon, ordered General Townshend on towards Baghdad. The Turkish forces, however, had prepared some excellent defensive lines. By the end of the first day, Indian forces had captured the first line of enemy trenches but losses had been very heavy.

On the second day of the battle, the Turkish army counter-attacked and though the British beat them off, once again casualties were high. On the third day, 24 November, General Townshend, seeing that his losses were so great, decided that he had to withdraw and consolidate his position. Seeing the retreat, the Turks attacked in strength. Fighting all the way, the British and Indian troops fell back to Kut. So terrible had the fighting been that British troops, unable to get their tongues around the correct pronunciation of Ctesiphon called it Pissedupon instead. The allied forces were now trapped in Kut and surrounded by the enemy.

Meanwhile, in Southampton this month there was another charitable event. Pupils from the Shirley School for Girls contributed walking sticks and other useful items for the troops on Trafalgar Day and, in addition, raised £7 1s 6d by selling flags.

German prisoners being marched through the streets of Southampton

December

The fighting around Kut continued into December with a siege situation beginning on the 7th. This would last until 29 April, 1916, when the British and Indians finally surrendered. A large number of men from the 1/4th, 1/5th and 1/7th Hampshires went into captivity.

The news was little better for the rest of the last month of 1915. On the 20th, British troops were finally evacuated from Suvla Bay. On the same day, the evacuation of ANZAC troops from the beachheads at Gallipolli began.

There was one final snippet of news for the citizens of Southampton to ponder over. A couple of days before the Gallipolli evacuations, Sir John French was replaced as Commander-in-Chief of the British Expeditionary Force by one of his army commanders, General Sir

Douglas Haig. Sir John formally resigned on December 18th.

In Southampton it was announced that a father and son, both of whom worked in the fire brigade, had joined the army together. The father, Sergeant A.J. Collins, had previously served fourteen years in the army. His son, in addition to being a fireman, was a valued member of the All Saints football team.

The year 1915 had been one of mixed fortunes, new weapons and, above all, heavy casualties. It was only to be hoped that 1916 would be different.

Chapter Five

1916

January

It can be said that 1916 opened well for the children of Southampton. Around 120 of them were entertained at the Portswood tram depot and the special guest was none other than Santa. The event also managed to raise £100 for charity. On the same day, a large group of wounded soldiers were also entertained, this time at the Albion Congregational Church.

In the country at large, something that would have great significance later in the year occurred on 5 January when the Military Service Bill was introduced in the House of Commons. This would require all unmarried able-bodied men aged from 18 to 41 to register for National Service. It was passed on 24 January and would eventually lead to conscription.

On 6 January, HMS *King Edward* left Scapa Flow to sail around the north coast of Scotland and eventually on to Belfast, where she was due to undergo a refit. She was never to arrive. At 10.47 am she struck a German mine off Cape Wrath. Fortunately, only one life was lost, a sailor who fell overboard whilst the evacuation was taking place. Three days after this, on 9 January, the last British troops were evacuated from Gallipolli.

In Southampton, the new female tram conductors were the first in the country to adopt a regular dress uniform, which consisted of knee-length skirts and puttees. They were no doubt able to show these uniforms off at the end of the month when Italy Day was held in order to raise funds for the Red Cross in that theatre of operations. In order to encourage giving, the flag sellers were all dressed in Italian national costume.

Meanwhile, there could still be some strange events on the front lines. It was reported that on one sector held by the British, the troops had started to sing *"When We've Wound up the Watch on the Rhine"*. This, of course, was actually a patriotic German song and, much to the surprise of the Tommies, the German troops close to the line joined in with the chorus. This revealed their exact position, which the British then shelled before attacking in strength, and wiping out the Germans.

February

It was in February that one of the bloodiest and costliest operations of the entire war opened. It was a ferocious German attack on the French lines at Verdun and so bloody was the conflict that the battle would become known as the mincing machine. The first shots were fired on the 21st of the month.

A recruiting campaign in the town.

Before this, on the second of the month, pupils and friends of Queen's College held a concert at St Barnabas' Hall in aid of the British Red Cross. There were many such fundraising attempts: entertainments for the troops, flag days and other activities in many towns and cities throughout Britain during the war. In addition to raising funds for various good causes they also helped to maintain morale and gave everyone the impression that, even in some small way, they were all "doing their bit".

There were signs of great kindness on a local level too. William Murray, the manager of the Palace Theatre, had advertised for a night-watchman. Though many men applied, Mr Murray gave the position to Patrick O'Brien, an ex-soldier from the Royal Irish Fusiliers who had lost an arm whilst carrying despatches between trenches at Ypres. For his bravery he had been awarded the Distinguished Conduct Medal. Although he was Irish by birth, after he had been discharged O'Brien decided to settle in Southampton. Interviewed by the press, Mr Murray had stated that it was his opinion that heroes such as Mr O'Brien should be found positions when they could no longer serve.

March

At the beginning of March, news reached Southampton of a naval encounter that took place on 29 February.

A German raider had broken out into the North Sea and a British fleet of four ships had been sent to intercept it. What the fleet could not know was that the German ship was the cruiser SMS *Grief* which had hidden armaments of five hidden guns and two torpedo tubes. In the ensuing battle, the *Grief* was sent to the bottom but so too was one of the British ships, HMS *Alcantara*, with the loss of seventy two lives. The worry for the citizens of Southampton was that many of the men on board were from Southampton and the surrounding area. Many families waited with trepidation for the dreaded telegrams to arrive.

More recruiting in Southampton.

4 March brought news that, in order to help finance the war, the third budget since hostilities had broken out raised income tax to 5/- in the pound. Better news was received on the 10th when it was announced that Portugal, Britain's oldest ally, had joined the allies and declared war on Germany. Eventually some 20,000 Portuguese troops would join their comrades in the trenches on the western front.

At the end of March, the issuing of a new medal was announced. The Military Medal would be awarded to personnel below commissioned rank for bravery in battle on land. Many men from Southampton would receive this award before the war was over.

April

In April, the names of the local men who had perished when the *Alcantara* was sunk were published. Amongst the first whose names appeared were Henry Wilton, Alfred Wyles, Thomas Bone, Godfrey Baker, Bertie Eyers, Frederick Tanner and George Miell. The names of some local survivors were also listed, including Charles Caine of 1 Gloucester Terrace, Shirley, and Frederick Baker, the brother of Godfrey.

This terrible news was balanced by the story of Corporal Henry William Nicholson, who prior to the war had worked on the Southampton trams. A married man of 100 Howard's Grove, Shirley, he was awarded two medals for his bravery, the DCM and the Croix de Guerre. He received the last award from the hands of no less a personage than Douglas Haig.

A small bye-line in the newspaper carried reports of the arrest of Roger David Casement, in Ireland, on April 20th. Until the outbreak of war, Casement was something of a hero to the British people. A member of the British Consular Service, he had exposed scandals in Africa and South America for which, in 1911, he was knighted. At about the same time, he retired from the consular service and took up the cause of Irish Nationalism.

Soon after Britain declared war on Germany, Casement travelled to Berlin, where he tried to persuade the German government to support an Irish rebellion against British rule. Finally, they agreed to assist the Irish rebels by sending them a shipment of arms to use in a planned rising. In fact, most of these weapons were useless and obsolete ones captured from the Russians on the Eastern Front and so Casement sent a message to his comrades in Ireland, warning them not to use the guns. The British authorities intercepted this message and used it to trace the shipment, which was seized. Shortly afterwards, Casement landed in Tralee Bay from a German submarine. He was captured within hours of that landing, and taken to the Tower of London, pending his trial for treason. Of much greater significance were the events of 24 to 30 April, when the Easter Rising, without the help of Casement, took place in Ireland.

May

The local fundraising events continued throughout May. In the middle of the month, infants from the Mount Pleasant School presented a programme of old English songs and dances to raise money for the local hospitals. Meanwhile, the Palladium at Portswood proudly offered for the entertainment of its patrons a new film entitled *An American's Home*, in which the United States was invaded by a foreign force. The film was shown twice nightly with a matinee each afternoon.

Heroic acts need not take place only on foreign soil and this was made clear by a report about William Read of Summers Street, Northam. He led the successful rescue of an exhausted man who was stuck in thick mud near Northam bridge as the tide slowly rose around him. This was not the first life William had saved, for a few years before he had saved a boy from drowning in the river Itchen.

A more humorous story was that involving Mr and Mrs Spray of Cranbury Place. They had sent out their three young sons on a small shopping trip but the lads had failed to return. In fact they were missing for a total of five days. It transpired that they had wandered off and ended up in London. They were found in the capital and returned to the bosom of their family, no doubt to receive a severe talking to.

There was good news from Europe on 8 May when ANZAC troops, many of them veterans of the Gallipolli landings, arrived in France to add their strength to the allied armies. Back at home, Daylight Saving Time, later to be known as BST, was introduced on the 21st in the hope that it would boost production. Four days later, on the 25th, the Military Service Act passed into law.

Back in Southampton a most moving ceremony took place on 23 May. At the outbreak of war many Belgians had escaped to Britain, some of them were wounded soldiers. Some of those soldiers remained in Southampton and a number of them died from the wounds they had received. These dead soldiers were buried together in a special plot in Southampton's main cemetery and now a fine monument was erected there. The unveiling ceremony was attended by many local dignitaries.

Another sad event was the report of the death of Corporal H.A. Attwood, the eldest son of Mrs Attwood of 12 Harold Road, Shirley. Corporal Attwood lied about his age when he had joined up in June 1915. He had now died in the Mesopotamian campaign, at just 17 years of age.

Though the citizens of Southampton could not know it, as they went about their business on the last day of the month, the greatest naval battle of the war was about to take place. The German fleet tried to break out of the British blockade and the two navies met at Jutland. Once again, many Southampton sailors would lose their lives.

June

A total of 250 ships took part in the battle of Jutland; 151 British, Australian and Canadian and ninety-nine German. Though the battle was a success in that it prevented the German fleet escaping and allowed British dominance of the seas to continue, the losses were terrible. The British lost three battle cruisers: HMS *Indefatigable*, HMS *Queen Mary* and HMS *Invincible*; three armoured cruisers: HMS *Black Prince*, HMS *Warrior* and HMS *Defence*; eight destroyers; HMS *Shark*, HMS *Sparrowhawk*, HMS *Turbulent*, HMS *Ardent*, HMS *Fortune*, HMS *Nomad*, HMS *Nestor*, HMS *Tipperary;* and 6,094 men killed. Once again, many households in Southampton waited for news of their sons, husbands and brothers.

Another patriotic Southampton family. This time it is the Martin family.

At the beginning of the month there was yet another flag day in Southampton, this time named "Our Blinded Heroes Day". Then, soon afterwards, the names of the first local casualties from Jutland were announced.

One of the earliest names was that of 1st Class Stoker George Ferry who lived in Granville Street. It was also revealed that his family had supplied nine other members of the family to His Majesty's navy,

On parade in Southampton.

consisting of his father, his brother and no less than seven uncles. Within a few days, more names came to be revealed.

From HMS *Invincible* was Alfred John Kinnard, who lived in Howard Grove and was a telegraphist on the ship. Also named from that vessel were C.J. Barnes, a gunner and William James Fyne, who was only 18 years old. From HMS *Black Prince* were William Taylor of Nelson Street and Charles Young, Frank Austin, Roy Gillibrand and George William Hellier.

There was, however, yet another shock to come. A ship that many people in Southampton viewed as being especially close to their hearts as she was named after the county was HMS *Hampshire*. She had fought in the battle of Jutland and had been damaged but after the engagement headed back to Scapa Flow and from there to Archangel in Russia with an important diplomatic passenger. As the weather was unduly rough it was decided that she would sail through the Pentland Firth, then along the western coast of the Orkneys. It was there that the ship hit a mine and sank within fifteen minutes, with the loss of over 600 lives, one of whom was the important passenger, Horatio Herbert Kitchener, the Secretary of War, who appeared on the famous poster appealing for men to join the army and who had raised a force of over one million men. Only twelve survivors were rescued from the cold and stormy sea.

It seemed as though the month of June had brought nothing but bad news, but soon the citizens of Southampton, and indeed most of the towns and cities of the British Isles, would be reading even more bad news because a massive battle was about to open in the neighbourhood of the River Somme in northern France.

July

July opened in Southampton with a well attended Red Cross Fete on the County cricket ground. A day or so later, some fifty wounded soldiers were guests of the Gladstone Liberal Club and on Wednesday, 5 July, some 1,200 of the poorest children were treated to a fun day out, where some excellent food was provided.

By then, of course, news of the battle of the Somme had become widespread but, at least in these early days, it was publicised as a great push into the German lines and readers would be forgiving for believing that a massive victory was in the offing. What the press were unable to say was that the opening day had resulted in 57,470 casualties of which 19,240 were fatal. It was, and still remains, the British army's bloodiest day.

More soldiers on parade before being sent to the Front in France.

Though there were many reports of local men killed, perhaps one of the most poignant was that of Captain Stanley Thomas Arthur Neil. Although he had lived in West Yorkshire, he was a son of Southampton and his father still lived there. Stanley was appointed adjutant of his battalion at the end of June. Five days later he was killed on the Somme.

London Road in Southampton during the Great War.

He was 27 years old.

The names of more casualties from the battle of Jutland were published. Thus, Henry Martin, William James Pennicott and William Othen, all Southampton men, were listed as dead. There was, however, another local casualty who took up even more column inches in the local newspapers.

Charles Algernon Fryatt had been

More German prisoners marching through Southampton on their way to internment camps.

Another picture of German captives in Southampton.

born in Southampton and his family lived at 22 Trinity Terrace in St Mary's. They later moved to Essex, where he married and fathered seven children. He joined the merchant navy and by 1915 was captain of the SS *Wrexham*. On 3 March of that year his ship was attacked by a German U-boat but the *Wrexham* made a remarkable fourteen knots and managed to evade the submarine. For this, Fryatt was awarded a gold watch by his employers.

By the end of that same month, Fryatt was in command of the SS *Brussels* when he was again attacked, by the U33, which surfaced and ordered him to stop. It was clear to Fryatt that his ship was about to be torpedoed but instead of merely waiting he ordered full steam ahead and attempted to ram the submarine, forcing it to crash dive. This event earned Fryatt a second gold watch, this time awarded by the Admiralty.

On 25 June, 1916, the *Brussels* was surrounded by five German destroyers and escorted to Zeebrugge and then finally on to Bruges. Fryatt's German captors read the inscriptions on the two gold watches and realised that this was the man who had tried to ram the U33. Though the submarine had not been sunk, Fryatt was charged with that offence. He was tried on 27 July and sentenced to death. At 7.00 pm that same evening he was shot by firing squad. The case caused widespread condemnation, especially so in Southampton.

August

August saw further entertainments for the wounded soldiers who were convalescing in the various hospitals in and around Southampton. At the beginning of the month a cricket match took place on the County ground between Southampton and Portsmouth Corporations and about 1,000 soldiers were able to attend.

On the third of the month, Roger Casement who had been arrested in April, finally paid the ultimate penalty for treason when he was hanged at Pentonville prison by John Ellis. His was the only execution for that crime during the war.

There were yet more listings of local men who had been killed at the front or at sea and two notices in particular showed the tragedy of the war, involving families who had lost two men.

The first notice referred to a father and son being killed. Walter Hallett of the Hampshires had just lost his life in France. His father, Frank, was lost on the *Alcantara*.

The second entry mentioned two half-brothers. Frank Jones of Cambridge Street, Shirley died when HMS *Invincible* had sunk. His family had already known tragedy when his half-brother Alfred Bishop was killed on HMS *Bulwark* when it exploded in November 1914. There were many other families who lost two, or even more, members and all that marked their suffering was a few lines in a local newspaper.

Some notices of loved ones lost carried a deeper meaning when people realised what was behind

Captain Fryatt who was shot by the Germans for trying to ram a U-boat.

them. Thus, for example, there was a short notice stating that Private Edward Walter Ragless was missing. He had gone over the top on the first day of the battle of the Somme on 1 July. Now there was a second notice stating that he had been listed as killed in action. Had his body now been found or would his remains always lie somewhere beneath the mud of a shelled French field?

There were more local men lost at sea in this month. On the 19th, the German fleet again attempted to break the British blockade. They were beaten back to port but HMS *Nottingham* and HMS *Falmouth* were both lost, including fifty-one men.

September

The month was filled with stories of heroism, loss and attempts to maintain morale on the home front. There were more stories of young children doing their "bit" by raising money for good causes. Thus the people of Southampton read of seven-year-old Cissie Johnson, who was the daughter of the Superintendant of the local Fire Brigade. She had collected the sum of £4 7s 6d, mostly in odd coppers, for the local hospital. The report stated that her collection weighed in at just under fifteen pounds.

Western Esplanade taken during the war.

More names of the dead were published. Private Benjamin Ryley of the Machine Gun Corps, a married man who lived in Rock Street, was killed in France. His mother, Kate, still lived in the old family home at 2 Anglesea Terrace, Chapel. A group of men from Bitterne were also listed as killed. Leading Stoker Arthur Charles Pralle was yet another who went down with HMS *Black Prince*; his parents Charles Edwin and Eliza Jane lived at 17 Balaclava Road. Private Harry Reeves of the Hampshires lost his life in France on 26 August and Private George Hillier was killed on his twentieth birthday.

Two local men were awarded Military Cross, a decoration instituted after the war began, right at the end of December 1914. The first was Second Lieutenant G.G. Gilbert, who was the Chief Preventative Officer of His Majesty's Customs at Southampton. The second award was to Company Sergeant Major Cooper, of 35 South View Road, Shirley. He had braved intense fire to rescue a wounded comrade who had been struck by shrapnel after a shell had exploded.

At the end of the month there was yet another flag day, this time to raise funds to supply a war hospital. No doubt the citizens of Southampton gave freely to support yet another worthy cause.

October

Occasionally news of a tragedy suffered by another nation made the pages of the newspapers. So it was that in early October readers were informed that on 4 October a French troopship, the *Gallia* had been sunk in the Mediterranean. Over 1,700 lives were lost.

The 8th of the month marked the hundreth day of the battle of the Somme and still there was no end in sight. Perhaps what upset people most was the suggestion that the entire campaign had started as little more than an attempt to relieve the tremendous pressure on the French at Verdun. Well over a 100,000 lives had been lost there and the French army was feeling the pressure. The opening of the Somme offensive focused valuable German resources away from Verdun and the French could now regroup and counter-attack.

More German prisoners of war, many from the Somme battlefield, were paraded through Southampton on their way to internment camps and again hundreds of citizens of Southampton stopped to take a look at the men who had, until very recently, been trying to kill Britons.

More local names of those who had made the ultimate sacrifice for King and country were published. Sergeant Joseph Charles Ricketts of the Royal Field Artillery who lived at 1 Bowden Lane in Portswood, was killed in action on 15 September, the day that tanks were first used in battle. So too had Private R. Todd who although he lived at 4 Shamrock Place, Victoria Street, served with the Gloucestershire Regiment. Another local soldier, Private W.J. Woodcock, of 69 Oxford Street was in the Devonshires when he was killed on 22 September. These were just a few from the seemingly unending lists of dead and wounded published in newspapers across the country.

One amongst many tragic stories was that of John Russell Crook, who was the grandson of a local man, also named John, who still lived in Northam. John Russell's parents, George and Margaret, emigrated to Canada before the war, but when hostilities broke out John was determined to fight for his old country. He enlisted in the Canadian army in March 1915 when he was just 15 years and eight months old. It was easy for John to lie about his age as he stood six feet two and a half inches tall. In October 1915, John landed in France and was killed in action on 19 August, 1916. He was still only seventeen years old.

One of the most touching stories, though, did not involve someone's name, or rank, but still managed to instil deep sadness. A photograph was published in the Southampton newspapers. It was a picture of an attractive woman and the only identification mark on it was the address of the studio where it had been taken: Express Studio, 21 Canal Walk, Southampton. That picture had been found by a Scottish soldier on the Somme battlefield and must have been lost by some local man who was, in all probability, lying dead somewhere on the battlefield.

Meanwhile, life went on. At the end of the month the Grand Theatre proudly announced that it would be showing a fantastic new film, *The Birth of a Nation*. It would start on Monday, 30 October and would be shown twice daily at 2.30pm and 7.30pm.

November

November began with another story of children collecting for charity. Two sisters, eight-year-old Ada Dyer and four-year-old Dorothy, managed to collect £2 3s for Sailor's Day. At about the same time, a disaster struck closer to home, this time by the hand of nature.

On Sunday, 4 November, the combination of torrential rainfall and a high tide caused terrible floods in the low-lying parts of Northam. Water rushed into hundreds of homes and so bad did things become that the Southern Echo started a relief fund.

An interesting story was told by a local man, Ewart Willsteed, who had been a driver trapped in Kut by the Turkish forces. He had now returned home and described conditions during the siege. For six weeks the daily ration had been just four ounces of barley bread and one pound of horseflesh. When the horses had all been killed, the men were forced to eat dogs, cats and rats.

At the end of the month fresh horrors were brought to the people of Southampton. It will be recalled that the *Britannic*, sister ship to the *Titanic*, was turned into a hospital ship at the beginning of the war. On the morning of November 21st she was off the Greek island of Kea with 1,066 people on board when she struck a mine. She sank after approximately one hour; but fortunately only thirty lives were lost. Many of those onboard came from Southampton.

News travelled slowly and when details of the sinking were published it was not known what the death toll would be. Initial reports listed a number of Southampton men who were missing and these included: Leonard George, George Bradbury Philps, Frank Joseph Early, and John McFeat. Two other men, H. Walton, of 18 Belvidere Terrace and F. Blake,

The *Britannic* as a hospital ship. She was sunk by the Germans.

of 96 French Street, were known to be safe.

When the news did finally filter through, it was not good. Though relatively few men had died, there were Southampton men amongst them. Henry James Toogood, who was aged 48 and Leonard George, who was only fifteen years old. George Bradbury Philps was lost at sea, as was 27-year-old John McFeat. Frank Joseph Early lost his life as had George Honeycott, who was pulled alive from the sea but had later died from the injuries he received. George left a wife, Alice, and two young children, two-year-old George Edward and Kathleen, who was only one.

Above Bar during the First World War.

December

At the beginning of December one more name was added to those who had died on the *Britannic*. Percival William White, of 28 College Street was lost. Two of his shipmates reported that they had tried to save him as he floundered in the water but it was all to no avail and they had to watch in horror as his body sank beneath the waves. Later this month all the survivors of the sinking arrived back at Southampton docks.

There was much political trouble in the country, again over the way the war was being handled. On 5 December, the Prime Minster, Asquith,

resigned and two days later David Lloyd George assumed the position. Perhaps of more direct interest to the people of Southampton was that new modern tramcars had arrived. They had more room and were much more comfortable than the old ones.

There was news of a local son who was doing well. John Rushworth Jellicoe was born in Southampton in December 1859. He was in command of the British forces at the Battle of Jutland and now he was appointed First Sea Lord. There was news of another promotion, though not of someone from Southampton. On the last day of the year, Douglas Haig was promoted to Field Marshal.

Southampton had one last problem to face before 1916 ended. At around midnight on Thursday, 21 December, a large fire broke out at the Bedford Brewery in Bedford Place. Thousands of pounds worth of damage was caused.

Chapter Six

1917

January

It appeared that Southampton was doing all it could for the many wounded soldiers who arrived back through the port. At the very beginning of 1917 the medical and nursing staff at the Royal Victoria Hospital at Netley were working as hard as possible to ensure that their charges were able to recover from some of the horrors they had endured on the various battle fronts.

Collections were constantly being organised and many of these were based around workplaces. Thus, the employees of the Imperial Tobacco Company sang carols over the festive season and raised £11 9s 6d for the Red Cross Society.

Two more tragic photographs had been found on the battlefields of the Western Front. Private W.H. Furness of the South Wales Borderers had found two such pictures, both with the name of the Express Studios, of

Netley Hospital where so many wounded servicemen were treated.

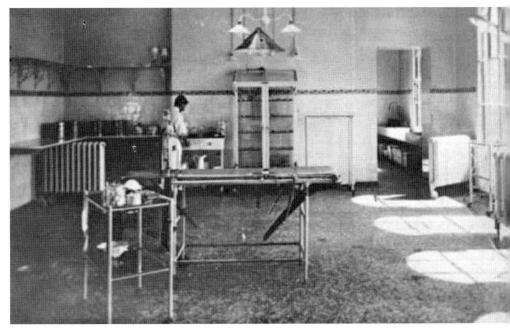

One of the operating theatres at Netley.

Canal Walk, printed on the back. One was of a young woman and the other was of two small boys. Had they been lost by a father and husband who would never return home?

Local entertainments were well attended. There was a baby show held at the King Street Mission Hall on 10 January and over the same period the Grand Theatre held its annual pantomime. This year it was *Sleeping Beauty*.

Many local people made their own entertainment, though. It was a particularly cold January and the lakes on Southampton Common froze over. Hundreds of people donned their ice-skates and showed off their abilities.

Whilst all this was taking place, secret German machinations were taking place on the diplomatic front. On 16 January, the German Foreign Secretary, Arthur Zimmerman, sent a telegram to the German minister in Mexico. The coded message asked that Mexico should come into the war on the side of the Central Powers, if the United States decided to enter on the side of the Allies. If Mexico agreed to this suggestion then Germany would offer as much assistance as would be necessary and would ensure territories Mexico had previously held were returned to her.

Unfortunately for Herr Zimmerman, the telegram was intercepted by British cryptographers and decoded. The message was then forwarded to the American government. The message read in part: *We intend to begin on the first of February unrestricted submarine warfare. We shall endeavor in spite of this to keep the United States of America neutral. In the event of this not succeeding, we make Mexico a proposal of alliance on the following basis: make war together, make peace together, generous financial support and an understanding on our part that Mexico is to reconquer the lost territory in Texas, New Mexico, and Arizona.*

The American reaction was one of fury. American citizens had already died when ships such as the *Lusitania* were sunk. Now Germany was implying that this situation might well recur and, in addition, were actively trying to get Mexico to wage war on their country. The Zimmerman telegram was to have far reaching consequences.

February

Heavy snow fell in Southampton in early February and a good-natured snowball fight took place between the boys of the Grammar School and Taunton School. Both sides claimed victory.

Unrestricted submarine warfare was indeed reintroduced by the Germans and one of the early casualties was an ex-German ship, the *Hanna Larsen* which had been seized in Southampton at the outbreak of war in 1914. Since that time she had been used to carry coal but now, on 8 February, she was attacked by U39 some twenty miles off Spurn Point. The same day, however, the U39 was intercepted by HMS *Thrasher* and destroyed. The Swedish master of the *Hanna Larsen* was a prisoner on board the submarine and was rescued by the British ship.

Meanwhile, the Zimmerman telegram affair was continuing to simmer. On 3 February, the United States severed diplomatic relations with Germany. There would be more developments in the coming months.

The cold snap continued and people were amused to see that a house in Winkle Street had a massive icicle formed outside. Coming down from the roof of the house the icicle was as tall as the house itself and had the girth of a well-built man.

There was an appeal by the government throughout the country for people to eat less bread. Supplies of grain were running low and it was believed that the new U-boat campaign would have a further detrimental effect on stocks.

The death was announced of Captain Percy Smith. He was a retired army officer who had taken no active part in the current war but was a survivor of the famous charge of the Light Brigade in Balaclava. He had been in the 13th Hussars, and was wounded by a thrust from a Russian lance.

Another local death was that of Captain J.A. Hewer, of 134 Pound Street, Shirley. He had fought bravely for his country and had earned some leave. He was on his way home to Southampton when he was killed in a train accident in France.

On the 25th of the month a significant German withdrawal began. All along the Somme front the troops gradually withdrew, sometimes as much as twenty five miles. It was not, however, some kind of tactical victory for the allies, though it was a consequence of the Somme fighting. The Germans were merely consolidating their positions and had pulled back to a strongly defended system known to the British as the Hindenburg Line. The withdrawal would not be complete until 5 April.

March

On 1 March, the contents of the Zimmerman telegram were made public in the American newspapers. The public reaction was vitriolic and there were public demands that American should declare war on Germany.

No sooner did it seem that Britain might gain a new ally than another fell into serious trouble. On 12 March a revolution took place in Russia. Three days later, on 15 March, Tsar Nicholas II abdicated and a provisional government was sworn in. The Eastern Front was now very vulnerable and seemed open to a successful German and Austro-Hungarian attack.

In Southampton more stories of families who had sent many sons to the front were detailed. One such was Mr and Mrs Brixey, of 44

A poster asking people to eat less bread in order to prevent shortages.

Liverpool Street, Bevois Town, who had five sons who had joined the forces. The sons were Albert, Charles, Peter, Harold and Frederick. Unfortunately, two of them had already been killed. Albert died in India on 14 May, 1916 and Frederick was killed in France on 1 February, 1917.

There was a most interesting sight for the people of Southampton to look at towards the end of the month. An ambulance that had been struck by a German shell at Verdun and been shattered, was towed through the streets and then put on display. It was, of course, then used to collect money for the British Ambulance Committee.

Women had, as has already been said, taken many jobs previously done by men so that they could be released for the forces; but now women too were given the chance to serve directly. On 28 March, the Women's Auxiliary Army Corp, or WAAC, was formed. Within days 57,000 women had joined and by 31 March, 9,000 of them were already in France.

Just before the end of the month another vessel carrying many Southampton men was sunk by a German U-boat. *The Asturias* was a hospital ship and had discharged around 1,000 wounded soldiers on 20 March. At about midnight, two torpedoes struck the ship. At the time there were a large number of female nursing staff on board and these were helped into the lifeboats first. It was reported that thirty-five lives were lost.

A typical propaganda poster from the Great War urging men to join the forces.

April

On 6 April the United States declared war on Germany and joined the allied cause. In time thousands of American soldiers would arrive in Europe and the Central Powers were well aware of that fact.

The list of men from Southampton who perished on the

Asturias was published early in the month. The list of the dead was:-

James John Tillyer of 60 Payne's Road, Freemantle

Charles Henty Hall of 1 Dock Street

Randolph Blair Lawes of 4 Malmesbury Road

Reginald Ernest Hunt of 19 Shirley Park Road, Shirley

Herbert George Kimber of Cobbett Road, Bitterne Park

George Robert Jones, aged 16, of 12 Chaplin Street, Highfield

W.D. Shaw of 53 New Road

James William Earl of 8 Queen Street

Harold Edwin Gerald Shore of 13 Western Esplanade

Stanley Henry Cross of 5 Winchester Place, Craven Street

Ernest HenryReeves of 14 Longcroft Street

Edward Thomas Baden Doncom of 88 College Street

Orlando William Green of 29 Duke Street

George Bevis Harvey of 95 Albert Road, Chapel

Percy Newton Tubb of 22 Marsh Lane

James George Alfred Munson of 71 Northbrook Road

Arthur Edward Brown of 9 Cross Court, Cross Street

Arthur Charles Andrews of 85 Stafford Road, Freemantle

John Albert White of 9 Floating Bridge Road

Victor Charles Mafeking Orman of 3 Laundry Road, Shirley Warren

Albert Isaac Kneller of 19 Bellevue Street

Henry Seymour West of Grange Lane, Netley Abbey

Robert Stone of 122 Radcliffe Road, Northam

Harold Thomas Stone of 6 Middle Road, Sholing Common

John Aitken Anderson of 9 St Mary's Road

Edwin Alexander Glasspool of 83 Bedford Place

The Germans also had propaganda posters urging their men to fight against the Allies.

Arthur Edward Humby of 48 Bullar Street, and John Bertram Ernest Robinson, whose address is unknown.

Out of the thirty-five men who had perished, twenty-eight came from Southampton.

On the wider European scene a number of battles opened in this month. On 9 April, the battle of Arras opened. The British advanced three and a half miles on the first day and Canadian troops captured Vimy Ridge. The battle continued to 4 May, and although land was gained, the losses in men were very heavy. There were also heavy casualties at the Second Battle of the Aisne, a mainly French offensive which lasted for four days. British troops were involved in another battle, that of Gaza where they were heavily defeated by the Turkish army.

In Southampton the Salvation Army opened a communal kitchen at Batterberg House for the benefit of the poorest people in the town and a local citizen started what was to become a new trend. Mr W.E. Kerwood, of 38 Melbourne Street placed a home-made memorial plaque of honour on the wall of his house, naming the seventy-seven men from his street who were serving in the forces. It was something that would be copied by people from other streets, who were equally proud of the efforts being made by those who lived nearby.

Another Military Medal was awarded, this time to Captain A.E. Jones. This was given extra coverage in the newspapers as Captain Jones had worked for the *Southern Echo* before he had joined up.

The story of Fireman Arthur John Priest, of Briton Street, was certainly uplifting as he appeared to have a charmed life. He was an engineer on the *Titanic* when it sank, the *Alcantara* when it went down, the *Britannic* when it hit a mine and had just been on another hospital ship which had also been sunk.

The month ended with some unforseen trouble on the Western Front when the French army mutinied around Chalons-sur-Marne in protest at the defeats they had recently suffered and the heavy casualties they had sustained. The mutiny would continue in one form or another until October.

May

On 18 May, the United States Congress passed a bill allowing the government to raise a new army of half-a-million men. Two days before this the local casualties in yet another sinking, that of the *Arcadian*, were listed. Another ten Southampton men had perished at sea.

In the same month there was yet another sign that women were being employed in what would normally have been regarded as men's work. In Totton, a group of women were now working as road sweepers.

June

On 7 June yet another battle opened in Belgium when nibeteen huge mines were detonated along the Messines ridge. Following this British, Irish, Australian and New Zealand troops attacked and seized the ridge, south of Ypres. The battle lasted until 14 June.

Ten days later, on 17 June, Portugese troops saw action in the front line for the first time but, perhaps of greater import, later in the month, on 28 June, the first American troops arrived in France. They would not see action yet as there was still much training to be done.

In Southampton, news of the loss of two brothers was given. Twenty-year-old Private Charles Edward Macey, of 1 Didcot Road, Shirley, had been killed in action on 18 November 18, 1915 and now, on 23 April, 1917, his brother, 23-year-old Lance Corporal Frederick William Macey was also killed. Both had been in the 2nd Battalion of the Hampshires.

There was also news of two men who lived in the same street and were killed. Private Ernest Churcher lived at 143 Pound Street in Shirley and was killed on 25 April. A few doors away, at number 155, lived Private William Parsons who died on 17 May.

July

The idea of setting up shrines in the streets of Southampton was spreading. In early July another was set up in Granville Street, which included men from Stamford Street, Marine Street and West's Place. There was a total of sixty houses in those four thoroughfares but the shrine listed the names of sixty-three men who were now fighting for their country.

The early days of the month saw some good news. On the 6 July an Arab force, led by T.E. Lawrence captured the port of Aqaba on the Red Sea.

One relatively small snippet of news was that the British Royal family had announced, on 17 July, that they had changed their surname from the

German sounding Saxe-Coburg-Gotha to Windsor. It had only taken them three years to realise that this would be a good thing.

Another huge battle opened on the final day of the month. People heard that a new attack had begun in Ypres, the third battle there. It came to be popularly known, however, by a different name, that of the village when the British attack ended. So it was that the third battle of Ypres was known to all as Passchendale and the fighting would last until 10 November.

August

Though it would not be reported at the time in the British press, the first signs that morale was failing in Germany took place on 3 August when there was a mutiny of the German High Seas Fleet in Wilhelmshaven. The British blockade of the seas had really begun to bite now and there was rationing in Germany. The coming winter would be known there as the turnip winter as there was little else to eat in some towns and cities. The German sailors were merely the first to show dissatisfaction with the way the war was going.

The first of August saw a new entertainment for wounded troops when a pageant of *Alice in Wonderland* was staged on the County cricket ground. The following week, on 8 August, the ground staged another event when a team of wounded soldiers took on a team of women munitions workers in a cricket match.

There was also news of a local hero gaining employment after being injured in the fighting. H.W. Bulpett, of 8 Magdalene Terrace, had lost an arm whilst serving in the navy. Invalided out of the forces he was now working as a constable at a munitions factory in Wales.

September

The type of war Britain and her allies were fighting could sometimes be brought home quite starkly. Thus in Southampton there was the story of Corporal W.F. Beale, who lived in Shirley. A rather casual report carried a picture of a strong looking young man, which had obviously been taken before he reported to the muddy trenches in France, for the article beneath mentioned that he was at home recovering at the moment as he had been wounded at Messines in June and subsequently gassed in August.

Yet another large scale battle opened this month, part of the continuing third Battle of Ypres. On 20 September British, Australian and New Zealand troops attacked along the Menin Road. Steady advances were made but again at a great cost in human lives.

October

There was another massive fire in Southampton at the beginning of this month. On Thursday, 4 October, at around midnight, flames were seen at Messrs John Gater and Co's flour mill at West End. The fire brigade attended but they could do nothing to save the premises, which were burnt to the ground.

British troops were involved in two major battles, in different theatres of the conflict. The Second Battle of Passchendale opened on 26 October, where the Tommy was joined by Canadian soldiers. Just five days later, on 31 October the Third Battle of Gaza took place. This was where the British had previously suffered an ignominious defeat but this time, finally, they managed to break through the Turkish lines decisively.

November

There was a most moving ceremony at Hampton Park on Sunday, 4 November. The event was organised by the Reverend Neville Stiff, the vicar of St Agnes, who publicised a gathering to commemorate the fallen heroes of the area. Emotional speeches were made and these were followed by a volley of shots, fired by a local unit. Finally, a single bugler sounded the Last Post.

This event was reported at the same time as the story of a local mother, who this year had lost three members of her family to the war. Lucy Kirby, of 16 Northcote Road, Portswood had lost her husband, Private Cecil Ernest Kirby of the Hampshires who had been killed on 1 August, 1917. She had also lost her son, Lance Corporal A.W. Purkiss of the Wiltshire Regiment, who had been killed in Mesopotamia on 18 January 18, 1917, and her brother-in-law, Private Ernest Edward Lee, who had been living with his wife Fanny, at Christchurch. He too served in the Hampshires and was killed on 10 April, 1917, in France.

Events around the world continued to fascinate the people of Southampton. On 7 October a second revolution took place in Russia. Led by Lenin and Trotsky, it overthrew the provisional government set up after the first revolution and put the Bolsheviks in power.

On 10 November the Third Battle of Passchendale ended with the capture of the village of that name but the seeming futility of operations on the Western Front was shown more vividly by events at Cambrai.

On 20 November, the British used tanks for the first time on a huge scale at Cambrai and in the ensuing battle had captured much ground there and advanced into the so-called Hindenburg line. This cost many lives on both sides, but was at least termed a British victory. Ten days later, on 30 November, the Germans counter-attacked and recaptured almost all of the ground they had lost, again at the cost of many lives. However, the attack proved that no matter how magnificent defensive lines might be they could be penetrated, if one ignored the number of human lives lost.

In April 1916 Southampton was told the gallant story of Corporal Henry William Nicholson, the tram worker who won the Distinguished Conduct Medal and the Croix de Guerre. Now the town was told that Nicholson, since promoted to second lieutenant, had been killed on 3 November, 1917. He left behind a grieving wife, Caroline.

December

There was great news on 9 December. British troops captured Jerusalem ending 673 years of Turkish rule. There was also news of a local man who had had a most fortunate escape.

Private Sidney Richard Courtney, of St Andrew's Road, had been fighting in France for nine months. Recently he had been wounded in the thigh but the bullet had then bounced off his food knife, meaning that little damage was done. He was now recuperating in a military hospital.

There was also the story of two brothers who served in the same unit and had fought side by side. Leonard and Vernon Curtis lived at Bedford Place and were fighting in France where both were wounded. Vernon, who had been on the staff of the Pictorial before the war, was now on two weeks leave with a relatively minor wound. Leonard had been less fortunate and had lost his left arm, but at least the two brothers were still alive.

On 15 December, after the second revolution was all but complete in Russia, a document was signed which must have caused the Allied commanders some sleepless nights. It was on that day that Russia signed an armistice with Germany and hostilities on the Eastern Front were suspended. Would this mean that thousands of battle-hardened German troops would now be moved westwards? Would they balance out the arrival of the fresh American troops and would this lead to years more of bloody warfare?

The year 1917 ended exactly as it had begun for the people of Southampton. A new snap of freezing cold weather meant that the local lakes froze over again. Once more there were people skating on the Common.

Chapter Seven

1918 The German Advance

January

The year opened with a sense of expectancy. Few people, perhaps, believed that this would be another 1917 with one battle after another leading nowhere and having little overall effect. There was a sense that this year, finally, something would happen to change everything. Of course, in Britain that expectancy was of an Allied victory. The people would just have to wait and see.

The losses in merchant shipping and other factors were leading to shortages of certain foodstuffs. Right at the start of the year, the Southampton Master Butchers' Association announced that, due to their inability to obtain adequate meat supplies, their shops would be closed on 2 and 3 January; and added that this closure might be extended even further. It was little consolation to read that there were similar, if not even more severe, problems in Austria and Germany. There were very severe food shortages in Germany, there had been peace strikes in Austria and civil unrest in Germany had led to the arrest of executives of the Independent Socialists in fifty towns.

Throughout the country there were "tank banks". These were attempts by various towns and cities throughout the United Kingdom to collect as much money as possible so that new tanks could be built. In Southampton, a tank named Egbert appeared in the town and by 4 January had raised £73,380. By the time Egbert left the town towards the end of the month, it carried with it no less than £141,000 from the citizens of the borough. Southampton could be proud that it was towards the top of the league for fund-raising only being surpassed by much larger cities such as London, Edinburgh and Birmingham.

There was still more local tragedy to report. Private George Edward Stratton who was serving in the Gloucester Regiment but who was a native of Southampton and lived at 42 James Street, was reported as killed in action at Cambrai, just eight days after he had returned to the front after being home on leave.

Despite the continuing war, the wheels of officialdom continued to grind and people still faced courts for various offences. On 11 January, the Southern Counties Dairy Company were summoned for selling butter at prices which exceeded the official maximum. It was stated that they had, in some instances, made an extra sixpence on a pound of butter. In their defence, the diary claimed that this had been due to the actions of a single branch manager who had acted contrary to their instructions. Found guilty of twenty-nine counts, the dairy was fined a total of £136. No doubt that particular branch manager found himself looking for another position.

Another case, heard on 24 January, was that of John Morley who was accused of unlawfully wearing a military uniform. Although from Southampton, he had joined a Lancashire regiment when he was under-age and had later been discharged due to ill health. Determined to fight for his country he had obtained another uniform, made his way to France and joined an Australian unit. He had fought in several battles, including Cambrai before being caught. He was remanded for inquiries but was treated quite leniently as his intentions had been of the highest.

February

There was another court case at Southampton on 1 February. Eighty-year old Mary Houlthan was accused of hoarding a total weight of sixty-five pounds of food for her own use. She pleaded guilty and was fined £4.

Food shortages continued to bite. On 3 February, a new instruction, the Public Meals Order, came into force and this had a direct effect in Southampton. It related to what could be served in hotels and restaurants. From now on, no meat could be served for breakfast and patrons had to take their own sugar into such establishments. Meat at lunchtime could not exceed three ounces and milk could only be supplied to infants and invalids. Finally, no patron might consume more than one and a half ounces of bread, cake, bun, scone or biscuit between 3.00 pm and 5.30 pm.

On 6 February the Representation of the People Act received Royal Assent and passed into law. This new Act meant that almost all men could now vote. More importantly, it also gave the vote to women over the age of 30. When the next General Election took place there would be millions of new voters.

On Saturday, 10 February, there was yet another flag day, this time in aid of shipwrecked mariners. At about the same time, the citizens were 'treated' to another entertainment by Fred Evans, a well-known cinema character, who gave a talk explaining what life would be like if the Germans won the war.

On 20 February, survivors from the torpedoed transport ship *Tuscania* arrived in Southampton to a large cheering crowd. Later they were treated to a gala performance in their honour at the Palace Theatre. Around 1,200 American servicemen attended the show.

An interesting case was heard in court on 27 February when Florence Holmes, a 21-year-old auxiliary post-woman, appeared charged with throwing some 400 letters into Southampton Water. She had been engaged on a temporary basis to cope with the extra mail over the Christmas period but, growing rather tired of delivering the items, had thrown a bundle of letters, cards and other items into the water. The bundle had later been found by a soldier, who passed them back to the Post Office. Florence was sentenced to pay a fine of £5 or serve one month in prison. She elected to pay the fine.

March

The Southampton Communal Kitchen was opened on Wednesday, 6 March, by the Mayoress. Situated at Back-of-the-Walls, it served the first customers the following day, 7 March, and did a roaring trade.

On 19 March, the local magistrates dealt with the case of James David Jackson, who ran an eating house in the town. He had been allowing his premises to be used for the purpose of betting, with the assistance of his fellow accused, Alfred Aubrey. These two had conducted a most lucrative business of betting on football matches and it was reported that during the previous season some £2,398 had passed into Jackson's bank account. Under the circumstances, the fine imposed, just £100, was perhaps a little lenient. Alfred Aubrey was also fined £50 for assisting in the commission of the offence.

A most unusual case was heard by the Southampton Coroner on 22 March. Mrs Eliza Louise Gibb, the wife of Commander Gibb, had slipped from a chair on which she had been sitting. A portion of her blouse had caught on a door knob on the kitchen dresser and she had been unable to extricate herself and, being partly suspended, was eventually suffocated. A verdict of accidental death was returned.

The day before this, on 21 March, the first sign that 1918 was to be a decisive year, occurred in Europe. A massive German assault, code named *Operation Michael*, was launched in the Somme and Arras area with the intention of splitting the British and French lines. It was initially a great German success and the British suffered very heavy losses and began a major withdrawal. The fighting would continue until 5 April, but there was worse to come.

April

The first day of April was a momentous one for Britain's airborne servicemen for it was on this day that the army's Royal Flying Corp was amalgamated with the Royal Naval Air Service to form a new body, the Royal Air Force.

On 9 April the Germans launched a second massive offensive, code named *Operation Georgette*. This time the point of the attack was the British line in Flanders. Again it caused many casualties and the Germans captured a great deal of ground, reaching ever closer to Ypres. The battle continued until 29 April and, for the first time perhaps, there were many who were beginning to think that the tide of the war was turning against Britain and her allies. Indeed, about the only newsworthy success at this time was the death of the famous German air ace, Baron Manfred von Richtofen, who was killed over the Somme on 21 April.

Whilst men were dying in their thousands on the battlefields a certain callousness was evident in another Southampton court case. On 29 April, Hetty Audrey Cooper was fined £20 for unlawfully wearing the uniform of a Red Cross nurse. She had used the uniform to collect money from local hotels and then pocketed the money herself.

May

In May, there was another large German offensive, code named *Operation Blucher* and aimed at the French and British lines around Chemin des Dames; the fighting lasted until 6 June. It was another successful campaign and the allies were forced to retreat a large distance. The Germans appeared to be winning the war. Yet, all three of these offensives had been held and the Germans had gained nothing much beyond territory which had already been devastated by war and earlier battles.

June

On 9 June, a fourth massive German attack was launched. This one was directed against the French lines south of Verdun, near St Mihiel and was given the code name *Operation Gneisenau*. It was another initial success, with more ground gained, but the bad news was tinged with some hope. During the fighting a number of German prisoners were taken and one, a German officer captured near Verdun, was interrogated. During that interrogation he volunteered the information: 'It is impossible for the war to continue much longer. Our losses are terrifying. My company lost 80 men out of 105. Germany is suffering too much. She cannot go on. We are all tired.'

In Southampton, where people were also tired and suffering, life continued. On the 27th the Pirelli Cable Works appeared in court charged with having some unfenced machinery, as a consequence of which a female employee had met with an accident. The poor woman had been so badly injured that she lost an arm. For this horrendous occurrence, Pirelli were fined the paltry sum of £25.

On 30 June a court case opened in Bootle, Merseyside; but it had a Southampton connection. Thomas Alexander Meek married in 1907 and he and his wife, Alexandrina, had two children. The marriage collapsed and Alexander travelled down to Southampton, where he married a local girl in March, 1917. He had not, however, bothered to obtain a divorce from his first wife and was now facing a charge of bigamy. He was held in custody pending a further court appearance.

On 28 June there was more horrific news for the people of Southampton to read. Yet another hospital ship, the RMS *Llandovery Castle*, was torpedoed by a submarine. The *Llandovery Castle* was acting as a Canadian hospital ship and was sailing from Nova Scotia to Liverpool when she was attacked off the coast of Ireland. This, though, was not the end of the matter. After sinking the ship, *Helmut Brummer-Patzig*, the captain of U86 surfaced, ran down the lifeboats with his submarine and machine-gunned the survivors in the water. Out of a total complement of 258 men and women on board the ship at the time, only twenty-four survived.

The first half of 1918 had been disastrous for Britain and her allies. Would the second half be any better?

Chapter Eight

1918 The Tide Finally Turns

July

On 4 July Southampton, like many other towns throughout the country was decorated in red, white and blue bunting to celebrate American Independence Day. It was a gesture much appreciated by the troops from America.

It was also at the beginning of the month that the alleged bigamist, Alexander Meek, who had married a Southampton girl, appeared in court at Bootle for the second time. Found guilty as charged he received a sentence of eighteen months imprisonment. His 'wife' returned to Southampton. She was never named in the newspapers of the day, but research shows that she was Rebecca Peters.

On 15 July, a fifth major German attack of the year was launched on the Western Front. Once again, this was aimed at the French line near the river Marne, but this time the usual big German advance did not occur. The attack floundered and it was French troops who advanced. The fighting lasted until 18 July. It appeared that the German strength had finally been sapped.

On the 18th, when the fifth German attack petered out, the Second Battle of the Marne opened. This was a French counter-attack, capitalising on their recent gains. Later supported by the British, the advance continued until 7 August.

The day after the German attack opened, news was received that in Russia, Tsar Nicholas II and his family had been murdered by their Bolshevik captors. The story appeared in the local and national newspapers a few days later.

Also in the local news were details of the death of Major Henry Wilfred Persee, of the Royal Fusiliers. He had been a member of the Hampshire County cricket eleven from 1905 to 1909 and lived at 48 Westwood Road with his wife, Marjorie. Henry was killed on 28 June.

August

On 3 August, the Australian hospital ship *Warilda* was transporting around 600 wounded soldiers from France to Southampton when she was torpedoed by the submarine U49 in the English Channel. It took the ship around two hours to sink and 123 people lost their lives, including many members of the crew. The significance for Southampton was not just that the ship was heading there, but that almost all of the crew were from the town.

Later in the month details of the casualties would be released including those of the death of one of the nurses on board, Violet Long. When the ship was hit, the crew had started to lower the lifeboats and Miss Long had fallen into the sea as she attempted to climb into one of the boats. Attempts were made to rescue her and it seemed that these had been successful but as she was half in and half out of another boat it suddenly swung against the side of the stricken ship and crushed her to death.

The *Warilda*, another ship sunk with the loss of Southampton lives.

One of the survivors, another nurse named Charlotte Allen Trowell, would testify to the bravery of the wounded troops. When the survivors were picked up by other ships, someone had called down for the wounded men to be lifted up first. They all immediately called out that there was a girl in the lifeboat and insisted that she should go up first.

On 8 August a second allied counter attack against the Germans was launched. A combined force of British, Australian, Canadian and French troops attacked the weakened German line on the Somme. Massive advances were made with the fighting continuing all along the allied front to the end of the war. By 13 August, the Germans were surrendering in droves and in three weeks the allies took over 70,000 prisoners.

September

Now one allied victory followed after another. On 12 September, there were battles along the Hindenburg line in one of which, at St Mihiel, American forces distinguished themselves.

On the 15th, French and Serbian troops attacked the Bulgarians at Salonika and made steady gains. This was followed on the 19th by the allies attacking the Turks at Megiddo. Another steady advance followed with the Turks being pushed deep into Syria.

On the 27th, at the battle of the Canal du Nord, a final successful breach of the Hindenburg line was made. The following day, 28 September, there was a strong advance from Ypres during the Battle of the Flanders Ridges and again the Germans were pushed back. The very next day, 29 September, at the Battle of St Quentin, yet another break was forced in the Hindenburg line, the fighting continuing until 2 October.

It was, arguably, the most successful month of the war, made all the sweeter on the last day of the month for, on 30 September, the Bulgarians agreed an armistice with the Allies. The first of the Central Powers had been defeated.

October

September had been a decisive month. It was clear that the Central Powers had lost their taste for war and that their armies were exhausted. It was time to press home the advantage.

On 1 October, British and Australian troops, supported by local Arab forces, captured Damascus from the Turkish army. Later they would go on to seize Beirut, Homs and Aleppo. Two days later the Germans put out the first feelers for an armistice, based on President Wilson's Fourteen Points plan of earlier in the year.

On the 14th, the Turkish government made the first overtures for an armistice but the allies continued with their efforts against their enemies. On the 17th, they opened the Battle of Selle and once again the Germans were forced back.

The end of the month brought even better news. On 27 October, Austria-Hungary asked for an armistice with the Italians and three days later, on 30 October, Turkey formally signed an armistice, which came into force at noon on the 31st. The second of the Central Powers was out of the war.

November

Matters came to a head in November. On the first day of the month, Serbian forces captured Belgrade. Two days later, German sailors mutinied at Kiel and on the day after that there were large bolshevik demonstrations all over Germany. Five days later, on 9 November, Kaiser Wilhelm II abdicated and Germany was declared a republic. Two days later, on 11 November, Germany signed an armistice with the Allies on

London Road in 1918.

Station Road in Netley, around 1918.

the Western Front, with fighting officially ending at 11.00 am. Amongst the last fighting on the last day was a Canadian action in which they recaptured Mons, where the BEF fought its first battle of the war in 1914.

In the same day that the war ended, and celebrations broke out all over the United Kingdom, various mundane events continued. In Southampton, 45-year-old George Lloyd, a stevedore on the docks, pleaded guilty to stealing four bottles of whisky and a quantity of tobacco, valued in total at £3. Since he had a long criminal record for petty theft he received a sentence of eighteen months in prison.

On 18 November, Albert Edward Seacombe, who was only 17, was fined £5 for wearing a military uniform without authority. The story was a strange one. Albert's sister had recently married a serving soldier whilst he was home on leave. Soon after the marriage she had fallen ill and her new husband was loath to return to his unit whilst his wife was sick. Albert had then volunteered to put on the uniform, go to France and report to his brother-in-law's unit.

After the war was over, the Town Council released some official statistics which showed just how important Southampton had been to the war effort. In the period from 9 August, 1914 to 16 November, 1918, Southampton docks had sent to France 7,000,000 men, 821,000 horses and mules, 14,000 guns and limbers, 110,000 vehicles, 3,500,000 tons of stores, supplies and ammunition and had handled a total of 16,600 ships.

High Street, Southampton, near the end of the war.

It was a record to be proud of.

On 21 November, elements of the German High Seas surrendered off Rosyth and thirty-nine submarines gave themselves up at Harwich. Two days later, President Wilson arrived at the port of Southampton on the *Olympic*, to start a brief tour of Europe. He left for London the same day.

There were, of course, many prisoners of war to repatriate to Britain and one of the first contingents arrived at Southampton on 26 November. They were 400 of the "Old Contemptibles" who had been taken prisoner after the Battle of Mons and also at Le Cateau during the retreat, in 1914. They were welcomed at the docks by the Mayor and Mayoress and marched through the town to riotous cheering.

The war had been won. It was time now to win the peace. At the end of November a General Election was announced. Southampton would return two members but there would be five candidates for those two seats. They were Major General Sir Ivor Philipps (Coalition Liberal), Mr W. Durley Ward (Coalition Liberal), Colonel E.K. Perkins (Unionist), T. Lewis (Labour) and F. Perriman (Independent Liberal). It would be interesting to know what effect the female vote would have.

December

On 1 December, the first allied troops entered Germany. Soon afterwards talks began on the exact nature of the peace agreement to be signed by the various combatants. In newspapers throughout the country there were calls that as Germany had caused the war, she must pay reparations for all the suffering and damage she had caused. The seeds were being sown.

The General Election took place on 14 December. A total of seventeen parties or factions ended up being represented at Westminster. The big swing was to the Conservatives but the various coalition parties would still form the government. The Conservatives themselves had ended up with forty-seven seats but the coalition parties holdings were:

Coalition Conservative – 332

Coalition Liberal – 127

Coalition National Democratic – 9

Coalition Labour – 4

Coalition Independent – 1, giving a total strength of 473. David Lloyd George was sworn in as Prime Minister on 15 December.

The newspapers throughout the country reported that women had flocked to the polls in droves, most of them voting quite early on. This was also true in Southampton, where the two successful candidates were Sir Ivor Philipps and Mr Dudley Ward, the two Coalition Liberal candidates.

The Great War had started with an assassination and, in one of the curious quirks of history, it ended with one. On 15 December, the President of Portugal, Major Sidonio Paes, was on his way to the railway station at Lisbon, waiting to catch a train to Oporto, when he was shot three times. He was dead before he reached the hospital. His assailant fared no better, for he was grabbed by the crowd and summarily lynched.

This time there were no consequences for the other nations of Europe. The war was over. Britain had a new government with a strong majority. There was much to discuss in 1919 if the peace was to be built upon.

Chapter Nine

The Hampshire Regiment

During the Great War, the Hampshire Regiment, the regiment most associated with Southampton, raised a total of thirty-two Battalions. These were:-

1st Battalion – Mobilised for war on 23 August, 1914 and landed at Le Havre. They were involved in a number of battles, which included: Le Cateau, the Marne, the Aisne, and Messines in 1914. In 1915 they took part in the Second Battle of Ypres. The following year they fought in the Battles of Albert and Le Transloy. During 1917 they were in the First and Third battles of the Scarpe, and the Battles of Polygon Wood, Broodseinde, Poelcapelle, and the First Passchendaele. The following year, 1918, saw them fighting in the First Battle of Arras 1918, and the Battles of Hazebrouck, Bethune, the Scarpe, Drocourt-Queant, the Canal du Nord, Selle, and Valenciennes.

2nd Battalion – They were in India at the outbreak of the war. They first saw action in the Gallipolli campaign, where they fought at Krithia and Achi Baba. They were moved to France in March 1916 and fought in the Battles of Albert, and the Transloy Ridges. In 1917 they saw action at the three battles of the Scarpe, and also at Langemarck, Broodseinde, Poelcapelle, and Cambrai. In the final year of the war they fought at Estaires, Messines, Hazebrouck, Bailleul, Outtersteene Ridge, the capture of Ploegsteert and Hill 63, Ypres and Courtrai.

3rd Battalion – Remained at Gosport for much of the war.

1/4th Battalion - In 1915 one company was besieged in Kut until they surrendered to the Turks. They saw no other action.

1/5th Battalion – As for the 1/4th.

1/6th Battalion – Spent much of the war in India. Landed in Mesopotamia in September 1917.

1/7th Battalion – As for the 1/4th.

1/8th Battalion – Embarked for Gallipolli in July 1915. Fought at Suvla Bay. Later evacuated to Egypt.

1/9th (Cyclist) Battalion – In 1916 they went to India from Devonport, where they remained until October 1918, when they were moved to Vladivostock to support the White Russians They remained there until November 1919.

2/4th Battalion – In 1917 the Battalion was in Palestine, where they fought in the Third Battle of Gaza, the capture of Junction Station, and the Battle of Nabi Samweil. In 1918 they fought at Tell'Asur, and Berukin. In May 1918 they were moved to France, where they fought at Tardenois, the Scarpe, the Drocourt-Queant Line, Havrincourt, the Canal du Nord, Selle, the capture of Solesmes, and the Battle of the Sambre.

2/5th Battalion – They were moved to Palestine in 1917, where they fought at the Third Battle of Gaza, the capture of Junction Station, and the battle of Nabi Samweil. In 1918 they were involved in the battles of Tell'Asur, and Berukin.

2/6th Battalion – Absorbed by the 5th Battalion.

2/7th Battalion – They were sent to Mesopotamia in September 1917, where they remained.

2/8th Battalion – Absorbed by the 4th Battalion.

2/9th Battalion – Joined the 225th Brigade and based in Lowestoft.

3/4th Battalion - Absorbed by the 2/8th Battalion of the Wessex Reserve Brigade and in April 1918 were based in Belfast.

3/5th Battalion - Absorbed by the 2/8th Battalion of the Wessex Reserve Brigade.

3/7th Battalion - Absorbed by the 5th Reserve Battalion.

3/9th (Cyclist) Battalion - Absorbed by the 5th Reserve Battalion.

10th Battalion - Formed as part of the First New Army. In 1915 they left for Gallipolli and fought at Sari Bair and Hill 60. In October 1915 they were moved to Salonika, where they were engaged against the Bulgarians fighting at Kosturino, the Karajakois and Yenikoi. In November 1916 they were moved again and took place in various actions in 1917 including the capture of Homondos. In 1918 they fought at the capture of the Roche Noir Salient, the passage of the Vardar River and the pursuit to the Strumica valley.

11th Battalion – In 1916 they fought on the Western Front at Guillemont and Ginchy. The following year they were at the Battles of Messines, and Langemark and in 1918 fought at St Quentin, and Rosieres. In August 1918 they took part in the advance in Artois.

12th Battalion – Landed in France in September 1915. Two months later they moved to Salonika, where they fought against the Bulgarians. Their first action was at Horseshoe Hill in 1916. The following year they fought at Doiran. The next year saw further action at Doiran, and they also took place in the pursuit to the Strumica Valley.

13th Battalion - Became the 34th Training Reserve.

14th Battalion – In 1916 they fought at the Ancre and Thiepval Ridge. They saw more action in 1917, when they were engaged at Pilkem Ridge, Langemarck, the Menin Road Ridge, Polygon Wood and the Second Battle of Passchendaele.

15th Battalion – First saw action in 1916, when they fought at Flers-Courcelette and the Transloy Ridges. In 1917 they were at Messines, Pilkem Ridge, the Menin Road and actions on the Flanders coast. They were moved to Italy in 1917 but then back to France, where they fought at St Quentin, Bapaume, Arras, the Lys, Ypres, Courtrai, and Ooteghem.

16th Battalion - Became the 96th Training Reserve Battalion.

17th Battalion – Formed in 1917 but spent the rest of the war in either Whitstable or Southwold.

18th Battalion – Formed in December 1916 and disbanded a year later.

1st Garrison Battalion – Formed in 1916 but in 1918 became the 19th Garrison Battalion.

51st (Graduated) Battalion – Formed in 1917 and first went to Canterbury. Moved to Ipswich in March 1918.

52nd (Graduated) Battalion – As the 51st.

53rd (Young Soldiers) Battalion – Formed in late October 1917. In January 1918 it was moved to Rolleston.

In all, the Hampshire Regiment received eighty-two battle honours and won three Victoria Crosses. It lost 7,580 men killed during the Great War.

Chapter Ten

The Aftermath and the Future

Politics and the Peace Agreements

The New Year started with social unrest in Germany. A movement, known as the Spartacists Revolt was behind riots and demonstrations all over the country from 5-9 January before the revolt was put down by the authorities.

On 18 January, the Peace Conference opened in Paris and it was there that the idea of nations forming together to ensure peace in the future was developed. This new body was to be termed the League of Nations.

The terms of the peace treaty were presented to Germany on 19 May and Austria on 2 June. They imposed considerable military restrictions on the defeated nations and the ceding of great swathes of territory to other, often newly created, nations. It was this that led the sailors of the German High Seas fleet to scuttle their ships at Scapa Flow as a protest, on 21 June.

There were a number of treaties with the defeated nations. The treaty of Versailles was signed with Germany, in the Hall of Mirrors at the palace, on 28 June. The treaty of Saint-Germain with Austria followed on 10 September. On 27 November, the Bulgarians signed the Treaty of Neuilly and the Hungarians signed the Treaty of Trianon on 4 June, 1920. The final treaty, that of Sevres, was signed with Turkey on 10 August 1920, and was amended considerably by the 1923 Treaty of Lausanne.

Almost from the beginning there was a major problem with these best intentions of the Peace Conference, for the United States refused to ratify the Treaty of Versailles and said they would not join a new League of Nations. This would greatly weaken any such organisation. Nevertheless, the League was formed and had its first council meeting, in Paris, on 16 January, 1920. The first meeting proper took place at the new, permanent home of the League, Geneva, on 15 November, 1920.

During this same period a sad ceremony took place to remember Britain's dead and missing of the Great War. On 11 November, 1920, the second anniversary of the Armistice, the Cenotaph was unveiled in Whitehall and the body of the Unknown Warrior was laid to rest in Westminster Abbey.

All of this happened on the world stage and much of it had direct consequences for the citizens of Southampton, but what of the town itself. What did the people of the town endure now that the war was finally over?

Sport

Southampton's football club was elected to the football league in the season 1920-21, playing in the newly formed Third Division. They would put on an excellent show in their first season, finishing second to Crystal Palace by five points and only losing seven matches out of forty-two. Their best result was a 5-0 drubbing of Merthyr Town and their worst defeat was a 3-0 loss away to Grimsby Town.

They fared less well in the FA Cup. In 1919 they were beaten 3-0 by West Ham in the first round, after a 1-1 draw at the Dell. In 1920 they did slightly better, losing at home 0-1, to Cardiff City in the third round.

The town had more success in boxing. A local hero, Joe Beckett, fought four times in 1919. In March he defeated the famous Bombadier Billy Wells in the fifth round, which gave him the right to fight Frank Goddard at Olympia on 17 June. The winner of that bout would then have the right to fight for the European Heavyweight crown. In the event, Beckett knocked Goddard out in the third round and was welcomed with a fantastic reception when he returned to Southampton on 19 June.

Joe Beckett, the Southampton boxer who fought for the European heavyweight crown in 1919.

There should have been a fight for the European title, against the Frenchman Georges Carpentier, again at Olympia on 2 September, but that had to be cancelled, almost at the last minute. A last minute replacement was hastily found, an American named Eddie McGoorty was substituted. Beckett knocked him out in the seventeenth round.

The long awaited title fight against Carpentier finally took place at the Holborn stadium on 4 December but Beckett's run of success was over. The fight lasted less than half a round and it was a defeated and dejected Beckett who returned to Southampton a few days later.

The Military

Just as Southampton had seen millions of men pass through on their way to France and other theatres of war, now it saw many others leave the port for their native lands now that the fighting was over.

On 28 March, large crowds assembled at the docks to witness the departure of the *City of Poona*, with over 1,000 Australian troops aboard, on their way back home. There were many other such emotional send-offs. On 10 May, the White Star liner *Olympic* left with 5,000 Canadian soldiers. The band of the Lancashire Fusiliers stood on the quayside playing popular and patriotic tunes.

On 10 May, the *Aquitania* finally sailed, after being held up by a seamen's strike. That had another 6,000 Canadian troops on board. In fact, the strike was still continuing meaning that there were no tugboats available. The captain of the *Aquitania* had to negotiate his way out to sea with only a few ropes slung from the quay to help him. It was reported as a daring and skilful act of seamanship.

There was, however, one departure, on 23 August, that caused different problems and this time it was of British troops. Three hundred men of the 2/7th Warwickshires and the 2/5th Gloucesters were due to embark for France but refused to go, believing that they were really being sent to Russia. The men spent the night in Palmerston Park and refused to budge the next day. Negotiations having failed, the authorities called in three companies of the Sussex Regiment from Portsmouth, who arrived in full battledress, bayonets fixed and with a number of Lewis machine guns. The protest was soon over and the recalcitrant soldiers were placed under arrest.

The Southampton Mutiny

In fact, there had been an earlier revolt amongst the armed forces in Southampton. In January some 5,000 men had taken over the docks and refused to obey orders. Troops were sent for and were issued with ammunition and were then assembled outside the large customs shed where the mutineers were gathered. A call was made for the men to surrender, after which their grievances would be heard. The men agreed and later complained that they had been told they were going on leave when they were actually being sent back to France. That was the reason they had mutinied.

Strikes

There were a number of major strikes just after the war had ended and many of these had a direct affect on the people of Southampton.

There was a rail strike, which started in early February 1919 and the worst effects were in London and the south. There was a complete disruption of rail traffic in Southampton and at one stage the only things moving on the rails were military ambulance trains maintained by volunteers and soldiers.

In March a miners' strike followed, though the worst aspects of this were in the north. It did, however, also have a knock-on effect in the south.

On 9 May, the seamen's strike directly influenced the town and all traffic between Southampton and the Isle of Wight was lost. This, like many of the other strikes, was a demand for an increase on the basic wage of £3 10s per week.

At the end of July nearly all the labourers working for the Council went on strike. The only exceptions were the tram workers and the electricity workers. Their grievance was that they had asked for a five shilling rise six months previously and the claim had been constantly shelved. Fortunately this strike only lasted one day and ended with the workers getting their five shillings.

A national bakers' strike followed on 6 August and shortages were such that there was rationing in Southampton. Now customers were only allowed to purchase six ounce portions of bread each day. This strike only lasted for four days.

Perhaps the most amusing of these strikes was one which was confined to Southampton. On 8 September a film, *The Elusive Pimpernel* was being made in Southampton and 400 people from the town were sent by the Labour Exchange for three days' work. A crowd scene was being filmed and all the extras were dressed in French revolutionary clothing when it was discovered that they were only wanted for one day and would therefore only receive one day's pay. When the director shouted action, someone in the crowd shouted, 'We want three days' pay', and a strike followed in which the French revolutionaries climbed on to the battlements of the ancient walls and called down to the people for support. The strike was settled the same day and the actors got their three days' pay.

Crime

In war or peace, crime was always there. One early report was of a crime on 17 February when the premises of a jeweller's, J. Hollis, were broken into late at night and items worth over £2,000 were taken. Unfortunately for the burglars, the shop was on the beat of an extremely vigilant police officer.

Constable Burgon was passing the shop when he saw that one of the windows had breath marks on it. He called for reinforcements, the shop was surrounded by officers and when the two thieves, Percival Rogers and Clarence Ford, appeared on the roof, they were arrested. All the stolen property was recovered.

In July, a young thief named William Henry Riggs, who also used the alias Charles Henry Miller, appeared before the magistrates charged with housebreaking and larceny. Pleading guilty, Riggs, who was only 16, bragged that he had once broken into five houses in one day.

Accidents and Deaths

On 6 January, a sad event took place in Mount Pleasant Road. Just after noon a steam tractor, towing two heavily loaded wagons, was proceeding down the street when a young boy, seven-year-old John Newton of number 87, decided that he wanted a ride on the back of the tractor. He climbed on to the coupling but was shaken off and fell under the wheels of the first wagon. He was killed instantly.

The weather at beginning of 1919 was rather cold and there was a great deal of fog about the town. On 13 January, two trains collided in fog between Hither Green and St John's stations. Two carriages were derailed but fortunately there were no serious injuries.

On 19 May there was a serious gas explosion in Southampton when a mains pipe exploded in the street, scattering concrete and metal into the air. Many shop windows were shattered and three people were hurt. One of them, a 16-year-old girl, was kept in hospital with a shattered thigh.

A tragic loss of two lives was detailed at the end of February when the inquest took place on Ada Mary Brown, who was aged 18 and her friend, 16-year-old Daisy Winifred Holloway.

The two girls were found drowned in a pond with their wrists tied together tightly. The day afterwards letters sent by Daisy were received by her mother and a workmate. The one to her parents read

'Dearest Mother and Dad,

Just a line to let you know that I am oh so tired of life, and so have put an end to my miserable existence. I have been nothing but a worry and trouble at home, so I know you cannot miss me as you did Rosie whom I hope to join soon. I am not alone in doing this thing. I don't think I should have the courage alone, but Ada is going with me.'

At the inquest, Mrs Holloway explained that Rosie had been a younger sister of Daisy's and she had died from consumption the previous year. Daisy had not been a trouble to her family but had been rather depressed after recovering from influenza recently. It was decided that the two girls had died in a suicide pact whilst they had been suffering from temporary insanity.

Another terrible occurrence took place on 5 April, when 22-year-old Lilian Martin accidentally poisoned herself with acetic acid. Her brother had poured some of the liquid into a mug intending to use it to treat his warts but Lilian had mistaken it for a harmless beverage and had drunk it down.

Another accident on 7 June claimed the life of 19-year-old Louisa Nutburne of 15 Lower York Street. She had been working on a farm at Nailsworth with her friend Elizabeth Thornby. The two girls had been collecting straw on a cart but when Louisa climbed on board the horse bolted and she was thrown to the ground, striking her head. She died two hours later.

More tragedy followed on 9 July, when a young man died because of a model boat. Louis Bowden was a native of Gloucestershire but in July was staying with his uncle in Waterhouse Lane, Southampton. He decided to sail his model motor boat on the lake on the Common but the vessel became entangled in weed in the centre of the lake. Louis took off his clothes and swam out but got into difficulties and started to struggle. A passing ex-soldier, who had been wounded in the war, went into the lake to save Louis but, by the time he reached him, it was too late. His body was recovered later.

A most curious death was reported in August when the body of Charles Hankins, a retired coal-merchant, was found in his bedroom. Charles kept his clothes in an old, heavy sea-chest and when he was found he was kneeling on the floor with his head inside the chest. It appeared that he had been looking for some clothes when the lid had fallen onto his neck and compressed it.

Life and death, commerce, finance, sport, politics, crime and punishment and the everyday business of life had passed back to a degree of normalcy in Southampton. There were many grieving families and many men and indeed women who would never return home but slowly life returned to a sort of routine.

There was hope for the future now. The guns had gone silent, the treaties had been signed and the surviving soldiers and sailors were returning home. The coming years would, surely, mean that all the sacrifice would be worthwhile.

Two US submarine chasers, awaiting orders to put to sea.

A US submarine chaser refuelling.

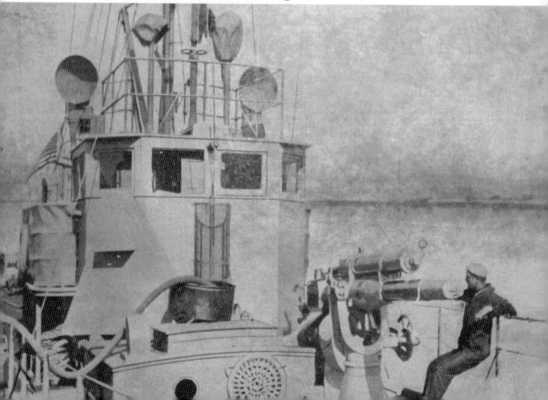

The USS *Melville*.

The United States Navy at Southampton, 1918

In 1918 the USS *Melville*, flagship for Vice Admiral William Simms, was docked in Southampton. The ship served as a tender to the American submarine chasers and carried 397 officers and enlisted men.

She left Southampton on 7 January, 1919, carrying US troops and heading for New York.

Bakers preparing jam pasties onboard the *Melville*.

Captain Pringle (centre) and his officers, aboard the *Melville*.

The reading room.

Huge loaves, baked onboard, stayed fresher for longer.

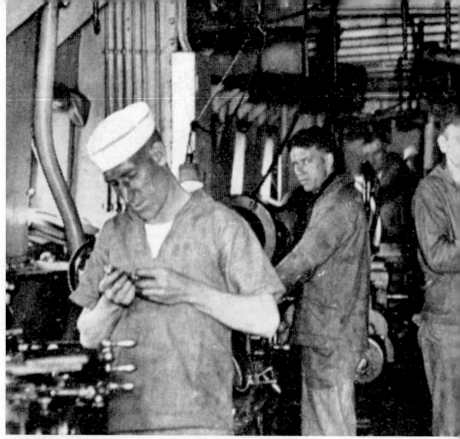

The *Melville* had its own machine shop and full complement of mechanics.

The men of the *Melville* enjoying some recreation time whilst ashore.

Being a supply ship, the *Melville* was well stocked with food. A carcass is butchered onboard.

Sailors of the *Melville* gathered aft.

The men of the *Melville* with their mascot, the ship's goat.

Index